BEST WISHES
M W

CW00865414

Surviving in the Theatre

A Biography of Michael Wheatley-Ward

From the Largest Theatre Group in the World to the Oldest Stage in England and the Future of the Theatre

Compiled by Michael Flagg

with additional ideas by Marnie Summerfield and Tom Cull

and edited by James Bellamy and Peter Such

www.newgeneration-publishing.com

New Generation Publishing

The Rationale for this biography from the subject himself -

Michael Wheatley-Ward

The reasons for this book being written are very simple. I will never forget the day in February 2007 when my Chairman of the Trust that owned the Theatre Royal Margate asked me to come and see him and it was not good news. In the presence of another Trustee he had written out a grim statement for me to read. Basically, that the Arts Consultants, put in at the suggestion of the then Manager of the Marlowe in Canterbury, had completed their task. It had been agreed that the theatre would be sold to the council, all staff made redundant and then re-opened as an art house with new staff in six months' time to compliment the new Turner Gallery in Margate. It also said that once re-opened the Marlowe in Canterbury would run the Box Office of the Theatre Royal Margate. My immediate reaction was I told you so, I knew this was going to happen, but how do I explain this to the staff?

I drove back to the theatre thinking about revenge but discretion being the better part of valour, I decided to await developments, as this project was most likely to fail, because the figures had obviously been manipulated. I recollected all the advice from theatrical folk over the years about 'stab in your back jobs'. The 'bluffologists' endemic in our society that cause disruption to pursue their own careers and leave a mess in their wake as they move on. The Trustees had confided in me that the Board were under pressure from the authorities to sell. I had initially supported the Turner Project but it seemed now to be kicking me in the face, although as a fatalist I could accept this as another example of doors in life opening and closing.

On walking into the theatre, I openly cried as I could not hide my emotions, but once having got the tension out of my system, I started the fight back. I noted that all the staff and Jay the technician, were not really that surprised and the lads in the office somehow knew from the expression on my face. The whole team were upset but we decided that we would stand together until the end.

I vowed to one soon-to-retire trustee and a local councillor, who still backs me to this day, that one day all this unpleasant business would be put into writing. The chance came when an unknown biographer, asked me to allow him to write my life story. Although I am not a big player in the theatrical business, here was an opportunity to put into writing all that is now available in one way or another in the public domain. Plus, with the assistance of a libel barrister, the presentation of this story as to be objective rather than subjective.

As you read on you will of course make your own conclusions but one thing I have learned from Bismark is to turn your defeats into victories.

Preface by Sir Alistair Hunter KCMG DL

Michael Wheatley-Ward epitomises British commercial theatre. He has spent most of his working life in the business, knows all its ins and outs, and is dedicated to 'bums on seats' – knowing his audience and putting on the shows they want to see. If he drops names, it's not for show: David Suchet and Julian Fellowes not merely agreed to be patrons of his current venture, they came to visit.

This is his story, told as a biography but with his own inimitable voice ringing strongly throughout. My own connection with him only appears in Act II, when he had been struggling for several years to keep the Theatre Royal in Margate open, and I became Chairman of the Trust which owned it; or part-owned it, which was the problem. The other owners would not cooperate in running the Theatre, and because of this dispute the Theatre got none of the public sector grants which are needed to keep a 200-year-old building in working order.

We alerted the Charity Commission, and within a year, using muscles that no-one knew they had, they had closed down the other Trust for irregularities and handed the whole Theatre over to us. At last, we were able to apply for grants. After a fierce 18-month negotiation, not only did we get the grants but the District Council bought the Theatre, which was an important step in ensuring its future preservation.

There was a price because the County and District Councils wanted a new programme with less box office and more community work, which they thought would appeal to their voters and justify their contribution. A new team would run it and Michael and his team, who had performed the miracle of keeping the Theatre alive for 15 years, were out. History had to be rewritten to support this. No longer was it a well-run theatre which had struggled for lack of adequate public support: it had become a badly-run theatre, saved for the community only by the Council cavalry riding to the rescue.

Michael must have been bitterly disappointed at being thrown off the project he had worked at so long and with such devotion. But he behaved with great dignity; took a deep breath and a short break; found a rather basic hall in the neighbouring town of Broadstairs which was unused four nights a week; and together with his old team, started a theatre there. Ever since, the Sarah Thorne Theatre has been showing them how it's done. For twelve years, it has been running a varied and high-quality programme of (mostly) professional theatre, including a traditional Christmas pantomime and an excellent four-week summer repertory season. All done without a penny of public money! Michael is now revered in the political circles where he was once derided, and his Theatre – and it really is 'his Theatre' – is an established and valued asset on the East Kent cultural scene.

Not a bad moment to look back on your life – and that's what he and his biographer do in this book, with gusto.

CONTENTS

The Castle Trust. Creation of a 'Friends Organisation' and a 'Club Licence'.

Introduction

Michael Wheatley-Ward could be described as a self-made businessman of the theatre who in his childhood days showed none of the academic promise of his father and sister. His learning-through-doing experience was based on 'trial and error' and 'reflective observation' (David Kolb Learning Theory 1974) which convinced him that he believes that much of what happens during life is determined by the hand of fate, often accompanied with a feeling of 'de-ja-vu!' Readers of this life history will discover that theatre buildings might have some connections with the paranormal, which some of Michael's experiences will suggest. Here they might encounter fascination as well as amusing experiences concerning some of the directors, performers, actors and cinema staff with whom he worked in London. Secondly, a reflective and objective account of his more recent local theatre management experiences, at Britain's second oldest theatre, the Theatre Royal Margate Kent, a Grade II listed building.

The focus in the earlier chapters is on Michael's formative years and reference is made to the London 'theatre village culture', which has also been an eye-opener for the biographer. Here is a rendition to appeal to the falling numbers of the local theatre-going public, although currently at the **Sarah Thorne** in **Broadstairs,** which he now manages with Jay Thomas, audiences are steadily growing. After the completion of three chapters of this book, Michael proposed the title, 'My Life Already'. However, on discussing this with a member the Terence Rattigan Society the response was, 'Well it is a good title but you are not Jewish! Much later when the book was almost complete, he hit on an intriguing description, **'How to Stay Solvent in the Theatre Business Without Trying'**.

In reality this book has evolved for two main reasons. Firstly, the subject felt flattered at the biographer's suggestion of the idea and secondly and more importantly, as an opportunity to address what actually happened at the end of Michael's tenure at the Theatre Royal. It is significant that there was no real opposition in principle to the Turner Centre by Michael, or the creation of such an art gallery as a loss leader and a means of putting an area in decline back onto the tourist destination map once more. Whilst acknowledging that some members of the public had been alienated to the idea of the Turner Centre from the moment it was mooted; there was agreement that something had to be done to kick-start the re-generation of Margate. (Michael felt that such a change to a mixed art display of contemporary and historical art, helped turn the corner for the gallery.) A further factor was job creation in an area of high unemployment and especially youth unemployment and the lack of opportunity for young people.

Reflecting on his own bumpy ride of work experiences during his early days in the theatre, Michael acknowledges that some assistance and direction is essential, although in his case he received no formal training except for the ABC's Theatres Management Apprenticeship Scheme. Personal experience has taught him that you will get there somehow through the 'University of Life' This is of paramount importance today as it ever was since a lot of the present-day young, in his view, appear to lack the good parenting with which he and others of his generation were blessed to assist them to develop their survival skills. He feels that cross-fertilisation with others and social interaction, can question your own aspirations, abilities and perceived disappointments. That being able to do this is an added bonus, regardless of whether or not you have supportive parents. Theatre students learn about character portrayal giving them an insight into character studies and human psychology, thereby enabling them to view and perhaps even empathise with the perspectives of others and even with those with whom they do not agree. Here is a process of learning psychology which can lead to changing attitudes in individuals and whole societies through questioning and challenging cherished beliefs. Throughout history the theatre has played so much a part in doing this even to the extent of sometimes offending some members of its audience. Helping students with the development of role portrayal, is also a means of recognising and nurturing their latent talent and raising their individual self-esteem and developing confidence. Putting it simply, in Michael's view, if you want to be an actor it is a 'dodgy business,' which requires a personal discipline as well as a dedication.

Furthermore, if you can't get a break in the professional theatre you can at least aim for a professional standard in the amateur theatre, whilst being economically supported. For example, in a work role, as say a bank manager or something else. Earning your own living to maintain economic stability, whilst enabling you to have a sustainable 'hobby'. Again, in Michael's view we need more people of this calibre in amateur societies or rather, 'semi-professional', which is the preferred term. It is disconcerting that the label 'amateur' implies people who don't know what they are doing which, of course, some might not, but not all. In the longer term this is an unfortunate perception for are there not after all 'amateurs' and 'amateurs', who may have professional standards for which they are not being paid, but who achieve their goals for themselves and others, through the love and challenges of the art? Another important factor is that drama students are gaining an education as well through learning by experience (i.e. experiential learning) often in an historical and literal context through studying say, a Shakespearian role and furthermore, as a team player and in a different time frame? Michael himself is an avid reader of history which he views as an education in itself. Participating in performing arts has similarities to the sporting world, requiring teamwork and there are many young and even older people who would be able to enrich their lives if they were willing and able to do this.

Michael enthusiastically continues to visit schools, colleges and other centres to explain and encourage the different ways of being involved in theatre, through set design, acoustics, front of house and theatre management, as he has done throughout his career. That performing in shows is not just in musicals, as most young people currently seem to want to do, but plays that ask vital questions about the problems people encounter in real life and how or could they be resolved. Local theatre can transport audiences to different cultures and time zones, not only for entertainment but for sharing experiences. The theatre of course about life itself, for after all is not all the world a stage?

Contemplating why someone should want to read this book and what the market for it is, could initially be merely confined to those 'theatricals' interested in the art. Although within these pages the reader will find some focus on local area politics, as a means of assessing objectivity and truth and what may have influenced the developments at say the Theatre Royal Margate, during his tenure as Director there. There have been many previous assumptions based upon rumour, supposition and lots of perceptions of 'daft projects' and money spent on them, in which the Theatre Royal has played a part. It would be good to think that the youth of today could benefit from learning about such a history of one of their local theatres and it might even encourage them to take a more objective and realistic view of their own personal aspirations in the theatre world.

When giving his lectures to pupils at schools, Michael emphasises that 'You may not know what you want to do but find an ambition and aim for the highest and you will pick something up on the way!' Once again this is a 'learning through doing' strategy and the feasibility of achieving certain aspirations. For example, although he always wanted to buy the London Coliseum because of his adoration of the building, in reality to own that old theatre you would need to be richer than Sir Cameron Mackintosh. Its greatest appeal to Michael is that it was Sir Oswald Stoll's masterpiece. This brings us back again to his early fascination as a young man in old theatre buildings, to be revealed in the chapters that follow in which Michael's comments should be taken under a 'without prejudice heading'.

CHAPTER 1- Not Following in My Father's Footsteps – but Developing a Personal Philosophy

My father was an only child and born when his mother was about forty. My grandfather was fifteen years younger than her and had been invalided out in the First World War. Father had shown considerable educational promise at school by winning all the prizes, becoming head boy and gaining a scholarship to the Queen Elizabeth School in Faversham. From there he went on to university. During the Second World War and on reserved occupation, he was involved with the development of items such as radio valves used in television, radar and the computer 'Colossus,' developed at Bletchley Park to encrypt German military messages. (1) Although he had chosen to go into education, I was later to discover that he and I had a mutual love of the theatre. I was born on January 20th 1950 in a nursing home at 16 Heathcote Grove, Chingford, Essex. My parents had moved from their furnished rooms in Ponders End, to a rented house at 2 Fairlight Close, Chingford. Renting a house was considered the norm in the 1950s and of course there was no central heating but coal fires and a gas Ascot boiler which had to be ignited to produce hot water. Mother, on having finished her war-time work in time and motion studies, became a housewife whilst Father went to work at Chingford County High School as a Science and Sports teacher. Finances were slim although my grandparents helped out which enabled my sister and I to go to the Normanhurst School in Chingford, a private school with reasonable fees. I remember on one occasion a mass of bills arrived leaving Father wondering how he was going to cope. This resolved me to never be in that position and my grandfather, who had his own shop, gave me the ambition to do the same, which I was later to do. Of course, I can remember our first electric kettle and refrigerator, the start of ITV and a new television so that we could receive both channels and later on I had a second-hand bicycle, all of which to a young boy was very exciting. Every year our summer holidays were spent with our grandparents at Faversham. We stayed over the shop, where Grandfather had opened and managed a branch of Curry's, which sold bicycles. Because of the lack of money to go too far afield we visited Whitstable, Margate and Ramsgate but I do remember these as being lovely holidays. Sadly in 1960, when I was ten years old, my grandmother died but we continued to stay with Grandfather for our annual six weeks summer holiday, which was glorious. There were two cinemas in Faversham – the Odeon and the Regal and I would spend Monday and Tuesday afternoons as well as Thursday and Friday afternoons watching different films. Wednesdays were half day closing and Grandfather would take us to one of the coastal towns. 'Saturday morning pictures' also operated and on Sundays we would visit my great aunt in Smarden. What wonderful times these were and I remember going to the cinemas with much fondness where my burning ambition actually began.

During this time rented accommodation was getting gradually more expensive as illustrated for example in the 'Rackman' era (1960), when some landlords charged excessive rents and exploited their tenants, some of whom were living in slum conditions such as in Westbourne and Notting Hill, London. My father had some savings and made the momentous decision to buy his own house, which was 23 Mount Echo Drive, Chingford, costing just less than five thousand pounds. Grandfather also helped out with a loan and Father now had a three and a half thousand-pound mortgage, which for him, was a frightful amount of money, but he thought that he had now arrived!

Mum and Dad

In 1961, as I had failed my eleven-plus examination, I went to the independent Loughton School for Boys, because my parents didn't like the idea of the local Secondary Modern School. My sister however, who was two and a half years younger, was academic and would eventually go on to university. I however was, like my mother, content with doing jobs around the house and never passing an exam; quite unlike my father. I wonder whether this could be an indication to others who fail their eleven-plus examination that they will not suffer irrevocably in the longer term, as for instance in the case of three school friends I know to this day. Roy Fraser, who went on to become a Senior Sound Engineer at the BBC and whose father flew Churchill during the Second World War. Paul Hough, who wanted to go into the RAF, but life took him via glider pilot training and he ended up being a senior pilot for British Midland Airways. His father was a director of several trust companies in the city of London. Finally, Andrew Baker who, like his father, was a brilliant pianist but followed him into the building trade. Andrew and I ran a pirate radio station named after one of our teachers called, **'The Fred Legg show'** . In addition to this Andrew 'modernised' the hymns in assembly and I will never forget his version of 'Holy, Holy, Holy' (in *allegro vivace*). Owing to the property market values increasing in 1962 Father expediently purchased a house at 23 Stanmore Way, Loughton, Essex which is on the edge of Epping Forest. I remember it was in this house that Father saw me crying on the stairs when I was about fifteen. On enquiring what was wrong I said to him, 'Father, I want to go into the theatre, I do not want to do any more education!' and this he accepted. From a very early age I had witnessed Father studying for his MA, whilst being employed as Head of Science at Tottenham Grammar. The amount of effort that must have been involved in undertaking his studies part-time, as well as carrying out his administrative responsibilities in his job, is unbelievable. Study and passing examinations must have been very important to him for he had a great determination to do this.

I also recollect as a child that we used to go past the old variety theatres, such as the **Hackney Empire and Finsbury Park Empire,** which I just had a natural affinity for, in that I felt drawn to them with aspirations of ownership. **The Hackney Empire** at 291 Mare

Street, Hackney, London E8, adjacent to the Town Hall was built by the renowned theatre architect Frank Matcham for Oswald Stoll and opened in 1901. **(2)** It was originally intended to be the Stoll Theatres' headquarters with offices and boardrooms until early on in construction Sir Oswald changed his mind by deciding to site his offices later at his flagship, the London Coliseum, which opened in 1904. Consequently, the front of the Hackney Empire had to be completely re-designed removing the intended office space. According to Ted Bottle, author of 'Coventry's Forgotten Theatre', the auditorium (featured next page) in 1988 had a curious colour scheme and the superb acoustics rendered it more akin to an opera house than a music hall or, as it later became, a 'House of Variety'. Music Hall artistes Marie Lloyd, Little Tich, W.C. Fields, Charlie Chaplin, George Formby and Max Miller played here and it has been used for concerts, drama, farce, cinema, radio and television recording.

Hackney Empire

Auditorium by courtesy of the Hackney Empire and Trip Adviser

Pictures by Ian Grundy-Permission of Hackney Empire Marketing Manager Rosie Curtis

The Finsbury Park Empire at St. Thomas's Road and Prah Road, London was also built by Frank Matcham for Moss Empires Ltd and opened on 5th September 1910. This was a centre for variety shows for a capacity audience of 2,000 and managed by Oswald Stoll. It was number two on the Moss Empires circuit, number one being the London Palladium. Finsbury Park Empire closed on the 7th of May 1960 and was demolished in 1965.

Finsbury Park Empire 1910 (Theatres Trust Archives)

Father took my sister and I to see shows, the very first being **'Little Goody Two-shoes'** with Jimmy Wheeler at the **Golders Green Hippodrome**. My father knew the leading lady, although we never found out how or why! I also remember this being in 1957, the year that Russia launched Sputnik 1.

12

Façade of the Hippodrome, Golders Green, circa 1916

THE HIPPODROME, GOLDERS GREEN

A Family Photo

For several years after that we went to Val Parnell's London Palladium where we saw a Morcambe and Wise variety show, 'Puss in Boots' and 'Old King Cole' with Charlie Drake.

Father also took us to the circus because my paternal grandmother, when she was in her forties, knew Bertram Mills, the circus owner, who used to winter at Smarden. In my youth, I wasn't overly keen on the circus for the simple reason that theatre was evolving within me, through making theatres in the garage and my sister and I used to put on shows. I remember I had a model puppet theatre made by putting an old blanket across the entrance to the garden shed and that it remained there permanently. This fascination for theatre obviously came from my father and of course my mother's father who built cinemas, so it must have been in the blood, but it had never actually showed in my father, as he was predominantly an academic.

When I was at the senior school, I found in the library a history of the London Coliseum by Felix Barker (published by Frederick Muller 1957). This was called **'The House that Stoll Built' (The Story of the London Coliseum)** (3).

Looking him up in encyclopaedias I discovered that I had the same birth date of January the 20th as Sir Oswald Stoll, the man who also built Moss Empires. Consequently, when looking up careers in the library at school this fact might have had some sort of significance which was to haunt me with the question, would I one day also be a theatre owner?

London Coliseum

London Coliseum Auditorium (Permission of Alamy.com)

Of particular interest for me was theatrical lighting and I recall a boy at school, who incidentally had bullied me until I eventually got the better of him. He asked me a technical question about stage lighting to which I gave an answer. He replied, 'You really ought to go into that, Michael, you know a lot about that subject ' Of course, all my knowledge, learning and experience had come through reading books and giving puppet theatre presentations. Also changing light colours using fairy lights, involving blues and greens and reds which are the primary colours. All of this was self-taught through writing my own scripts to doing my own shows. I remember one year that I had 'Dr Faustus' coming out from under the floor of the stage in the garden shed and I had a magnesium flash. There was a bit too much of it and I nearly burnt the shed down in the process, so perhaps here was an example of dangerous in-built intuition. A lot of the ideas for the puppet shows would have come from the BBC Puppet Theatre television programmes that I would also enact for the family and in which my father especially showed much interest. When I was twelve, I wrote to Eric Bramell who had the Harlequin Puppet Theatre at Rhos-on-Sea, Colwyn Bay, North Wales, in order to obtain a script he had written. His was the very first permanent puppet theatre in the UK, founded in 1958.

In the Daily Telegraph 6th August 1960, Jessica Salter had written an article about this small **Harlequin Puppet Theatre** in Rhos-on-Sea North Wales, built by Eric Bramall, stating that it was now run by his former partner, Chris Somerville, who in addition to operating the puppets was the box office manager and usher as well! **(4)** As an avid reader I often frequented the library and on one occasion found a wonderful book which I call 'the bible' by Frederick Bentham of Strand Electric, entitled **'Stage Lighting'**, first published in 1950 **(5)**. Although much of it is advanced physics, the basics are there. I studied it at school when setting and operating the lighting for school productions and the teachers knew of my interest. It also seemed to be a natural way to enter into the theatre. I obtained Eric Bracknell's book **'Making a Start with Marionettes'**, (Published by G. Bell 1960) from the library and renewed this weekly for a whole year until the librarian naturally got fed up and told me that I would have to buy a copy. My sister, who also had an interest in the arts, was destined to become a chemist and a physicist and was to follow in Father's footsteps to university. Sadly, in 2011 we were to lose her through cancer which also dragged Father down. More significantly, through perusing the family records and conversations with Mother, I found out that I had more in common with her medical history than my father, who later also developed cancer. For instance, I have high blood pressure, as does my mother, although she is now approaching 95. Back again to my earlier years. Father thought that his best investment was the garden shed which I called the 'Macabre Puppet Theatre,' because it kept me amused for years and did not cost very much. When doing the stage lighting I used the coloured sweet wrappers that mother discarded from her boxes of Quality Street to colour the lights. I even made my own puppets, as well as their costumes.

Family Name and Family Origins

People have often asked me why I am Michael Wheatley-Ward because I was christened Michael Ward. My parents didn't know whether to call me Miller-Ward after my mother's family or Wheatley-Ward because on my father's side his mother's maiden name was Amy Wheatley. I was privileged to make my own mind up what my name should be through deed-pole when I was eighteen. The Wheatley's and the Ward's actually finish with me since I have no children of my own although, I am privileged to be a godparent of eight. Mother and Father had met during war service in Enfield and started going out together and married post-war when they went to live in furnished rooms in Durance Road, Ponders End. My mother's mother, Granny Miller, was the daughter of a Methodist Minister and loved hearing Sunday evening hymns of praise and like my father's mother, she had also been a governess. Grandfather Miller was in the early motor car industry in Birmingham working for Lucas as a draughtsman and was later promoted to Chief Electrical Engineer for Lanchester Motors, which was then a serious rival to Rolls Royce. Surprisingly, he also built temporary cinemas and had a love of photography. He was offered a job by Henry Royce to take over electrical work at Rolls Royce in Crewe, but at the same time was offered a senior position at RAF Farnborough.

Granny Miller, being psychic, said to him to take the R.A.F. it's safer! At Farnborough Grandfather Miller worked on various projects with Barnes Wallis, including the spotlight settings for the Dam Busters raid. He also designed the electrics on most of the main RAF planes during the Second World War, including the Spitfire, Hurricane, Wellington and the Lancaster bomber. Because of the secrecy required he did not realise what he was actually working on until after the end of the war! He told me that he did not know that he had been working on the 'Gloster Meteor Jet', which was the first British Jet Fighter and the Allies only operational jet fighter; until one flew into Farnborough. A late uncle told me that one of his aircraft switches was seen in the rocket control unit on the NASA space project, but how true this is I do not know.

My father's parents came from farming stock, although my paternal grandmother was a governess and Grandfather Ward, an apprentice for Curry's Cycles, later to become a big electrical chain. He opened the shop in Faversham in 1920, and stayed there until retirement in 1963. He founded Curry's Group Servicing (TV repairs) at Faversham and was area manager for East Kent in the Second World War. He became the longest serving member of staff in the company and amassed a considerable number of shares, which was to serve him very well when Dixon's took the entire group over. His father, my great grandfather, was one of the founding agents for the mighty Prudential Assurance Company.

Some Further Family Reflections

Mother had applied to join the Wrens during her war service but failed her medical, which she always reckoned was due to her feet, although it was not exactly clear as to why. In consequence of this she went into time and motion studies in factories such as 'Vickers' at Weybridge Surrey and Edison Swan Electric Light Company at Brimsdown Ponders End, who made lamps with cellulose filaments. She was extremely self-reliant, having been the eldest of five children and having had to look after the family from a young age. Father maintained that his lucky number was 121 which was also the number of the television valve he designed, which used to keep the picture vertical on the TV, as well as being the new bus route he had campaigned for between Chingford and Enfield. He became the science and sports teacher at Chingford County High School, Nevin Drive, after the war ended and in 1948, he was promoted to Head of Science at Tottenham County Grammar School, which meant that he had to have a car to get there. Teachers were coming out of the army and Father would have liked to open a private school, but during these austere times this was not possible due to financial constraints. I remember going to my grandmother Ward and having to put up with a tin bath. My first Hornby train set was from my grandfather's shop in Faversham and had come from Curry's at a knock-down price. One year Father undertook extra teaching hours to take us on holiday to the Mount Stewart Hotel, Colwyn Bay, near Eric Bramell's Puppet Theatre.

My sister was born in August 1952 and I remember that after the Coronation in 1953 Father drove us up the Mall. There were still lots of bomb sites and Mother reiterated her early life in 1940 walking in London after the Blitz, as we travelled around St Paul's Cathedral. On Coronation night I stood at the end of Epping Forest at North Chingford, to see the face of Her Majesty the Queen in fireworks.

Peter Clark was a local lad whom I used to play with and he was the number one son to the King of Siam in a production of **'The King and I'** by Chingford Amateur Operatic, who staged their shows at the **'Scala Theatre'**, off Tottenham Court Road.

The Scala Theatre Auditorium -By online permission of Mathew Lloyd, http//www copyright Arthur Lloyd.co.uk 2018

Outside the Scala Theatre (Theatre Trusts Archives)

It never occurred to me that I would also later be involved with 'Am-drams', although my father was a great comedian and fond of Max Miller, whose shows he and Mother used to go to in their courting days. He was also a lover of 'Hancock's Half Hour' and 'Beyond our

Ken' during the 1950s. I also recall Father taking me to see Jules Verne's **'Twenty Thousand Leagues Under the Sea,'** in December 1954, a film which I became extremely fond of. When I was twelve, I read in The Sunday Times colour section about actress Sally Miles and Gerald Frow, a writer, who were married and were taking on the Theatre Royal Margate. Later, when on a school educational visit to Margate, a teacher asked me what I was doing during my holidays and I boldly replied that the family were restoring the **Theatre Royal Margate**.

On reflection, I realise now that this must have been some sort of premonition, for I thought I had told a lie, but was actually foretelling my own future. In cinemas and theatres I always felt at home and also had an affinity with churches, as they can be avenues to experience ghosts and spirits. (Chapter 6) As to religion I was baptised Church of England but never confirmed.

Forming A Personal Philosophy

I have always been an avid reader of history including **'The Rise and Fall of Communism,'** from which I learned that had Tsar Nicholas II been more liberal, Russia would never have had communism at all. There is always something to be learned from the mistakes of the past including bible history, especially the persecution of people of various faiths during the Roman Empire period. My interest in history probably developed from watching films which provided that stimulus. The Jews always seem to have been persecuted and although I am not one myself, I have always been welcomed by several Jewish families. I have a belief in a power we call 'The Lord' and until anyone can tell me otherwise I'll still expect 'someone' to be there if in a crisis. I find it comforting to pray in any religious place for the worship of God and the most peaceful place I have ever found myself in is the **Montefiore Synagogue**, in Ramsgate. There are so many strange things that have happened to me throughout my life, because doors have been opened as well as closed along the way. For example, I knew we were coming to an end at the Theatre Royal Margate in 2007, but had the faith to know that another door would open, which it did. It is as I had been removed from some dodgy situations so there must be some protective influence. Whether this is a spirit or a 'guardian angel', I cannot be certain. I have had many rewarding discussions with priests and vicars, which makes me believe that there is a power somewhere although I cannot explain what it might be.. I do not belong to any political party or anything which is power-based and am a self-taught diplomatist. From my studies into history I discovered that the Right Honourable Lord Louis Mountbatten of Burma (uncle to Prince Philip and second cousin to Queen Elizabeth II) did listen to others but made his own decisions. At Christmas 1962 Father gave me a copy of **'Theatres of London'** by Mander Mitchinson which became my bible. At school I could not get on with geometry and I never saw the point of algebra, although I remember later being on a 'Grand Master' lighting switchboard at the Phoenix Theatre London and writing out the theorem of Pythagoras because I was so bored. Was this really the proof that it had been learned by my brain but not understood? I could not even see the point of percentages which I can now do in my head for box office returns. For me I had to have a purpose for learning anything, although I enjoyed learning tables which in those days were memorised through being chanted by rote. I did pass one examination and this was the London Commerce Elementary Arithmetic Examination which pleased my father. He did not believe in gambling money or taking risks and was a firm believer of Paul Getty's directive, 'Never go into business for more than you can afford to lose!'

I never enjoyed acting, except in front of the bank manager, so might these be regarded as Oscar winning performances, I wonder? I was a bit shy as a kid but the theatre brought me out of this which maybe is a recipe for others to follow. The house in Stanmore Way, Loughton was adjacent to Epping Forest where I spent idyllic days, never having any pocket money but always finding things to do. From an early age I adored the stories of Charles Dickens and Rudyard Kipling. I also enjoyed opera, visiting museums and reading many topics of history, including Brunel's Great Western Railway, which has never left me. Nearer to home I remember the big Harrison Gibson's fire in Ilford where Mum and Dad had bought furniture.

Dad was convinced it was 'Jewish lightning' (slang for arson) for insurance. Always in my memory is 'The Room at the Top' where they had cabaret after the store was rebuilt.

Michael at Fifteen

References

1. Colossus

1943 and 1945 designed by an engineer Tommy Flowers. The prototype 1 being developed in 1943 and the Mark 2 version operating at Bletchley Park in February 1944. These machines enabled the Allies to gain a vast amount of enemy military intelligence messages between the German High Command and their army commands in occupied Europe. Consequently, this saved thousands of lives. It has been stated in error that Alan Turing used probability to aid cryptanalysis of the Enigma code, but it was Alan Turing's electromechanical bomb and not colossus which did this.

2.The Hackney Empire

The main owners of this building were faced with a retrospective planning order because during the restoration of parts of the building they had removed some of the original features including the external Terra cotta domes. Internally there is a grand vestibule and double staircase in marble, a lavish 1,500 seat auditorium with three boxes at the rear of the dress circle and either side of the auditorium.

3. The House that Stoll Built (The Story of the London Coliseum) by Felix Barker runs to 256 pages and was published by Frederick Muller. ASIN B00071Z8MU. Felix Barker is the author of several notable publications including 'London in Old Photographs', 'London 2000 Years a City' and 'London as It Might Have Been'.

4. The Harlequin Puppet Theatre Rhos-on-Sea
Today opens for seasons and especially during school holiday periods, at three p.m. and on one or two evenings at eight p.m. It is a Grand Puppet Circus that includes characters from the nineteenth century as well as tales from Brothers Grimm, Hansel and Gretel and a fantasy ballet originally devised by Eric Bramall who is now deceased. One of his protégés, Chris Somerville, has gained an international reputation for marionette manipulation and now runs the entire operation.

5. Stage Lighting

Frederick Bentham (1911–2001) is considered the father of modern entertainment lighting and became well-known during his 42 years with Strand. He was born in Harlesden in north-west London on 23rd October 1911 and joined The Strand Electric and Engineering Company in 1932. He made his mark by overhauling the product range, publishing a new case-bound catalogue in 1936 which included a host of innovative products such as mirror spots, acting area and pageant lanterns and the Light Console. This enabled superb lighting control and the ubiquitous 'Pattern 23 spotlight', became synonymous with Fred Bentham and Strand. The purpose of the lighting console was to progress the technology from a complex on-stage mechanical device to a remote control which could be located where the operator could actually see what was being lit. His reputation grew after the Second World War on taking over the editorship of Strand's popular journal Tabs. This was also combined with regular lectures and colour music demonstrations gained him a wide following as the focus of the industry's progressive developments. Strand's development team, under Fred's direction, was at the forefront of thyristor dimmer design, profile spotlight developments and ultimately, memory lighting systems. He continued his connections with the industry into his '80s, publishing his autobiography 'Sixty Years of Light Work' in 1992.

Chapter 2 - From First West End Job to Assistant Theatre Manager

As a consequence of my crying on the stairs in the Loughton house and wanting to go into the theatre, my father approached a friend who was a school careers advice officer. However, like my father, he had no idea of how to do this other than through acting because there were no institutions at that time for teaching theatre production management. He did contact an administrator at **'Theatre Projects'**, which was a stage lighting design company, who had their own theatre productions and even got me an interview in June/July 1965. At their London office they sat me down and said that they would offer me a job in their technical department if I got a few G..C.E's to safe guard me for the future and would I like to think about it? However, because I was so keen to leave school and get into what I perceived to be the 'university of life', I thought what do I do now? In the spring of that year I had been to the Theatre Royal Stratford East to see **'Widowers' Houses'** by George Bernard Shaw. (1) In which Phyllida Law, mother of Sophie and Emma Thompson, played the maid. (2) Having been to this lovely old theatre before as it was fairly local, I wrote to them to see if there were any vacancies and I received a reply from Buddy Woolsey the Chief Electrician on 28th August offering me an interview. I went along and as I could operate lighting switchboards, I was given a job as an electrician. My father said to me 'treat it as a holiday job because if you don't want to go into it you can still go back to school in September'. Well I completely forgot he had said this and in early September, when I saw all the children going back to school, I had this strange nervous feeling, perhaps psychic if you like, which developed further during the journey from Loughton station on the central line to Stratford. When I eventually stepped onto the platform at Stratford station, I knew that I had cut the umbilical cord and was now in the big wide world of work and that I actually loved it!

Theatre Royal Stratford E15 (Courtesy of Theatres Trust)

The Theatre Royal Stratford East opened in 1884 (3) and was owned by an actor manager Charles Dillon who, in 1886, sold it to Albert O'Leary Fredericks, his sister's brother-in-law. Fredericks added side extensions and later expanded the stage. Frank Matcham the well-known architect, made minor improvements in 1902 to the entrance and foyer and the Fredericks family management continued until 1932. A touring company which produced the pantomime **'Alice in Wonderland'** in 1950 returned as **'Theatre Workshop'** in 1953 under the management of Gerry Raffles and Artistic Director, Joan Littlewood specialising in new writings and ethnically diverse plays. **(4)** Apart from carrying out private work for Gerry Raffles I also worked for Stage 60, who rented the Theatre Royal from 1964 to 1966 under **'Pioneer Theatres'**. The total capacity of the house was 460 seats on three levels. Much later in the 1970s the development of the shopping centre would mean that this theatre would become threatened, but saved by English Heritage, designating it as a Grade II listed building in 1972. In 1965 Stage 60 had been working on a new play by the Nigerian author Wole Soyinka, **(5)** called **'The Road'**. He was the biggest author and considered the greatest play-write in Nigeria and became the first black African to be awarded

28

the Nobel Prize for literature in 1986. Not surprisingly there were many Nigerians in the audience and I had to go straight into this production as my first job with limited knowledge of the lighting procedure. Although I had no formal qualifications other than proficiency of the three 'Rs,' I was accepted as a standard electrician as it was considered I had sufficient knowledge to know what I was doing for which I was grateful, being at a tender age of only fifteen going on sixteen. Of course, there were no Health and Safety Regulations at that time and the acceptable age for the job was actually eighteen. I stayed with them after 'The Road' ended and then in the autumn of 1965, they mounted a musical play that ran from October 18th for twenty performances only as a 'fringe production'. It was called **'Something Nasty in the Woodshed'**, based on a line in the very successful novel by Stella Gibbons, 'I saw something nasty in the woodshed!' from **'Cold Comfort Farm'**. (6)

As is usual with some organisations that have been funded by the Arts Council, of which this was one, I discovered that they had budgeted completely wrongly and in this case the director wouldn't listen to the production manager who had overspent. It did attract audiences and I remember Peter Bridge the producer coming and paying a £1,000 option on the musical to take it into London but it never went anywhere. On the 28th October I received a letter from the management to say that as they were in serious financial difficulties, all contracts were being re-negotiated and the theatre went dark. This was my first taste of reality in theatrical life of which I was to become so accustomed to later on. I just accepted the situation feeling that there were reasons for it and an actress friend whom I had met on the stage of the Theatre Royal was of similar mind. Her name was Marion Park whom I still know and I remember we were both philosophical about it.

Ceiling of the Auditorium of the Theatre Royal Stratford E15-Theatres Trust Archives

**Recent Picture of the Statue Honouring Joan Littlewood's tenure at this theatre
1953-1975**

The theatre went dark before the next production which had originally opened here and came back from being on tour. This was the Joan Littlewood production of **'Oh What a Lovely War!'** Joan Littlewood and Gerry Raffles, had become owners of the Theatre Royal by buying it from the Fredericks family.

After 'Oh What a Lovely War' had closed I was assisting with removal of part of the set for storage in the auditorium space, when Gerry Raffles offered me and the other electrician money if we would participate in theatre maintenance and renovations until the next show came in. Miraculously this meant that we would continue to have a job. Gerry Raffles was a financial genius and a shrewd businessman who preferred to work in the theatre, keeping Joan Littlewood viable as theatre director. They had existed on minimum subsidy very well. Although Joan was a well-known socialist, she and Gerry having bought the theatre became the landlords, which always made me laugh. **'A Christmas Carol'** came in from the Watford Palace Theatre for Christmas 1965. Of course, what I could not know then was that Ray Lonnen, who was playing Bob Crachit, was later to be my leading man in my own first production company. At the Theatre Royal Stratford, I also worked with a young actor Nikolas Grace who went on to later fame in **'Brideshead Revisited'**. We kept in touch over the years and he was to help me find my director for my first tour in 1984. Incidentally, the Watford Palace Theatre is still a professional theatre today.

Watford Palace Theatre (Theatres Trust Archives)

Although there would be general work around in 1966 my mother told me to go and sign on to get money from the Labour Exchange after Christmas 1965. I wasn't proud but I didn't really feel I wanted to do this and when I did, they told me that because I had been paying self-employed stamps, I wasn't entitled to anything.

Consequently, I existed for a couple of months on the savings I had managed to accumulate or any work at the Theatre Royal Stratford East. Buddy Woolsey, the chief electrician, was also looking for work and had turned down the offer of a props man and offered it to me instead. This is how I managed to get my first West End job at the Shaftesbury Theatre in what became only a week's work for the ill-fated musical **'TWANG'** based on Robin Hood, with words and music by Lionel Bart and directed by Joan Littlewood. The intention of this show was to ridicule the crusades and the attitude of the church at that time, as well as champion the outlaw Robin Hood as a hero. The cast included Ronnie Corbett, Barbara Windsor and James Booth. However, the satire was considered by the critics to be too vague and in-consequential. On the production side dissension occurred during its creation, between Joan Littlewood, choreographer Paddy Stone and designer Oliver Messel. The rehearsals were disorganised and the atmosphere tense. Lionel Bart was apparently on a downward trend at this time and was alleged to be taking LSD. Some of these problems were leaked to the press which resulted in Joan Littlewood leaving the production. Burt Shevelove, an American, was brought in as a replacement director to make amendments to the score causing further confusion in that certain scenes, had little or no relation to the songs, which confused the actors. A Birmingham try-out was cancelled although one did take place at the Palace Theatre Manchester with an incomplete script. Lionel Bart was convinced he could save the show, but unhappily after the transfer to the Shaftesbury Theatre London on 20th December 1965 it closed only a month later, on January 29th 1966 against a background of bad press notices. On the first night the musical director Ken Moule collapsed with exhaustion having failed to completely orchestrate the second act. The production was played for camp and transvestism, with house lights going up and down during the first performance against a background of some vicious arguments backstage. There were some successful musical sequences including an around the gallows section, which turned into a Morris Dance around a maypole and some praise for Barbara Windsor. However, the tragedy of it was that it resulted in the loss of Lionel Bart's personal fortune and he was naturally devastated.

For me although it was dire, I did meet Barbara Windsor, Ronnie Corbett and other members of the cast who had been keeping the fight going. Bernard Delfont listed as a producer, had taken his name off the show because he did not want to be associated with it. All I can remember was that it was not only bad but lacked any co-ordination. Certainly, if today's people such as Cameron Mackintosh, had been approached to back it, they would never have touched it with a barge pole. In my view here was a total dependence on Lionel Bart's and Joan Littlewood's name because it involved all the old **Theatre Workshop** artistic team.

There was another show that came into the Theatre Royal Stratford East called **'Sweet Fanny Adams'** by Stephen Lewis (who played Inspector Cyril "Blakey" Blake) in **'On the Buses'**, who was a charming man and nothing like the 'thick-o' he played on the TV show. This production had a wonderful cast including Ronnie Barker who was a great chap to talk to, together with a lot of old Theatre Workshop people including the actor George Sewell.

Incidentally, George Sewell's cousin Con Watkins who came to visit the cast, was the plumber at the Coliseum where I was later to work. Brian Murphy, who in this production was playing a barman in an East End pub in the docks, was a bit of a joker and he said to George Sewell, 'Can you do a walk on?' George Sewell replied, 'Yes, I'll just come on in the middle of the play'. So George Sewell came in and strolled up in a drunken manner saying, 'Where's the urinal?' to which Brian Murphy replied, 'How many funnels has she got?' Apparently, I was the only person who laughed at this as I found it to be an amusing play. Judy Cornwell, noted for her role in the British sitcom as **'Daisy'** in **'Keeping up Appearances'**, was also in the cast. Sadly though it didn't go anywhere, not even on tour. You could see that the Theatre Royal Stratford East was heading for closure, not necessarily due to the lack of audiences but the lack of proper management. Stage 60 had gone bust in 1966 and Gerry Raffles and Joan Littlewood were looking around trying to decide what to do with the theatre next. As a consequence of this, I was to receive advice from an old stage hand Fred Waite, whose wife Florie Waite was a well-known wardrobe mistress. He worked on the railways at Stratford which was a better income than being in the theatre and he said, 'You had better join the union NATKE!' That was the National Association of Theatrical and Kinematic Employees. So I paid my subs and I went up to London and it was here that I made my only political contribution ever in my life. I have still got the union card as evidence. I paid 2/6d a week in arrears and 6d political levy which my mother has never forgiven me for because she became a staunch Tory, although her father was a Labour Party man. However, I actually got exemption from paying this levy in the end and on joining the union, I was offered several jobs in London. One was at the Globe Theatre that required boiler work as well as being an electrician, which I didn't really fancy. It was called a 'day-man' required for stoking the boiler as well as doing the electrical work.

Later in 1966 I went for a job interview at the Palladium with the chief electrician who had heard of my father probably during his school years at Tottenham Grammar, as deputy headmaster. When I told him my age he said, 'Ah, I can't take you on at the Palladium until you are eighteen. You've got the experience I need, so when you are eighteen come back to me and I will find you a job!' He later made a phone call to my father verifying this promise. Meanwhile I went back to the union to see what other vacancies were available and one came up at the Phoenix Theatre, controlled by **Prince Littler,** an English theatre proprietor, impresario and television executive born in Ramsgate Kent as, Prince Frank Richeux (1902–1985 – information from Wikipedia). He had an elder sister named Blanche with whom he had started a theatre company in 1927. He produced Ivor Novello's, Glamourous Night in 1936, Learner and Loewe's Brigadoon in 1950, Rogers and Hammersteins Carousel in 1951, Frank Loesser's Guys and Dolls in 1953. Offenbach's Can Can in 1954, George Mitchell's the Black and White Minstrel Show (1958) and Sheldon Harnick and Jerry Boch's Fiddler on the Roof in 1966. **The Phoenix** with a capacity of 1,000 seats was built in 1930 on the site of the old Alcazar Music Hall which had later reverted to a gambling house. The builder Sidney Bernstein was the founding chairman of the Granada group. In 1965 it was owned by a film producer and his wife Gerald and Veronica Flint Shipman. (7)

Here Noel Coward had his début with the very first production of his play **'Private Lives'** on 24th September 1930. Much later between 1968 and 1973, **'Canterbury Tales'** had a long and successful run there.

The chief electrician who interviewed me said, 'You are a young man and I will give you a helping hand because people have helped me. You can have the job as the Assistant Electrcian'. So in May 1966 there I was in the West End at barely sixteen on £18 per week, having previously been on £9 per week at the Theatre Royal Stratford East. I had doubled my salary although I now had the additional expense of getting into central London.

Phoenix Theatre by Courtesy of Theatres Trust

However, The Phoenix was 'dark' at this time for tax reasons because what **Prince Littler** did with his West End theatres was to group them into separate companies. Prince Littler's main company **Stoll Theatres Corporation** owned as subsidiaries **Moss Empires and Associated London Theatres. The Phoenix Theatre** was owned by 'HM and S Limited' (i.e. Her Majesty's and Shaftesbury Theatre). The old Shaftesbury 1,196 seat theatre was built by John Lancaster in 1888 for his wife Ellen Wallis a Shakespearian actress and was located on the south side of Shaftesbury Avenue east of Gerrard Place. It was bombed in 1941 and never rebuilt but the Princes

Auditorium of the Phoenix Theatre (Theatres Trust)

Theatre was the last to be built on the corner of Shaftsbury Avenue and New Oxford Street was bought by EMI in 1964 and changed its name to **Shaftesbury Theatre**.

The old Shaftesbury was situated near the Palace Theatre and they had their leases under **Her Majesty's Theatre**. When I went to the Phoenix in May 1966 it was 'dark' having a lease with Her Majesty's which was doing very good business with **'Fiddler on the Roof'**, but the Phoenix was coming to the end of its lease. Consequently, it was necessary for tax purposes, for the Phoenix to be dark. The first show came in the summer of 1966, which was HM Tennant's **'Lady Windermere's Fan'** by Oscar Wilde. Michael recollects that ironically just as this show came in, the Australian technician had a job offer back home and left. Consequently, Michael put forward the name of the chap who had helped him at Stratford East Buddy Woolsey, as a possible replacement. They took Buddy Woolsey on – he and Michael were working together again.

Anthony Quayle, the director of this production, was a wonderful chap and very polite and gracious to me. I was absolutely smothered with big names at this time. Jo Davis, the world-famous lighting designer who worked for Marlene Dietrich, had just finished **'My Fair Lady'** at the Theatre Royal Drury Lane. On seeing me he must have known that I was under age but he just said, 'We'll go through it, Michael!' He was well-known for complicated lighting plots, although fortunately for me this was a standard play. It was very noticeable that he adapted the requirements to enable me to operate on the 'Grand Master' switchboard, which was not electrically controlled or computerised. There were two people with me as I was operating the central handle to mechanically manoeuvre the dimmers with a guy either side of me, locking them into position. I had to do the master fade up and down by using a central wheel. This was one of the last theatres in London using this system and nearing the end of its lease so they didn't want to spend any money on the more modern boards which were now available. I remember it was very hard work like a 'galley slave' but I loved it! Fortunately, the play was properly lit throughout and it all came together.

I also remember at this time going into the box office one day and meeting Hugh Beaumont known as 'Binkie Beaumont', the legendary producer. Because I was a young man and he was an 'old queen' I dare say that there was a fascination on his part. **(8)** Another thing about that production was that I got to know very well Juliet Mills, the eldest daughter of John Mills and Mary Hayley Bell and who had begun her career as a child actress. Her aunt Annette Mills, had played the piano for **'Muffin the Mule'** for the Children's' Television broadcast from Alexandra Palace between 1946 and 1952. Incidentally, she is associated with Broadstairs as she at one time lived in Dumpton Gap. **(9)** I also remember her sister Haley, coming on stage one day.

For Wilfred Hyde-White, also in the cast of **'Lady Windermere's Fan'**, we had to put in special heating because he always felt the cold and one day, he asked me to go to his dressing room to talk about it and I was so in awe. I just remember a pile of one-pound notes he used to give out for tips, but as he put his hand out to shake mine, I was stupidly so nervous that I could not reciprocate. I was befriended by other cast members, Coral Browne the Australian actress and Isabel Jeans. Coral Browne used to come in most nights and say 'where's my little fucking electrician?' I had to go to her dressing room naively thinking it was for chats but she obviously thought otherwise. At that time, I also bumped into Vincent Price who was courting her. She was very kind to me as was Isabelle Jeans. At the Phoenix I also struck up a friendship with Isabel Jeans' dresser Melanie Rowlands, who had just finished on **'Funny Girl'** as personal dresser to Barbra Streisand, whom she described as absolutely charming to work with. Years later my mother confessed to my new wife Terrie, my father had worried about me working in the West End at the age of sixteen, because I might get involved with an actress! Sadly no, but the fireman at the Phoenix did try it on one night. He had been at the battle of Jutland.

There were always fascinating people in the audience for **'Lady Windermere's Fan'**. One night there was a memorable speech where Isabel Jeans has to say 'my dear nieces – you know, the Saville girls don't you, such nice domestic creatures – plain, dreadfully plain but so good – well, they are always at the window doing fancy work and making ugly things for the poor, which I think is so useful of them in these dreadful socialistic days.... and this terrible woman has taken a house in Curzon Street, right opposite them - such a respectable street too! I don't know what we are coming to!' (Duchess of Berwick Act 1 from Lady Windermere's Fan). This particular night she really banged her stick down and nearly broke it and got tremendous laughs and we wondered why. Harold Wilson, the Labour Prime Minister, was in the audience.

Wilfred Hyde-White attracted visitors galore and I remember being told to hold the lights one night and we were five minutes late going up after the interval. Who should walk across the stage, look up into the box and say 'Thank you for holding it', but Earl

Mountbatten of Burma! You could see that although he was a bit pompous, he was royalty and also in charge as he had a commanding style about him. Sir Malcolm Sergeant turned up another night and it was a wonderful experience for a sixteen-year-old in the West End and I doubt if you will see those days again as such people kept coming and going. The production team that Binkie Beaumont used included everyone who had worked on **'My Fair Lady'**, so we were getting visits from that cast and one night we were entertained by Stanley Holloway as well as one of Binkie's boy friends in the production who played the butler and tried to befriend me.

'Lady Windermere's Fan', was to be the final production of Prince Littler's at the Phoenix and he wanted it to be a good one. It terminated on the 18th March 1967 and the theatre then changed hands, the lease reverting back to the landlord Flint Shipman. It had been a fascinating time although closure after 200 performances meant another period of darkness which took in Christmas.

During the run Wilfred Hyde-White had been on £700 a week, but his limited contract had run out and his part was taken over by Douglas Byng, a pre-war Danny La Rue. After about a week or two, I was standing outside the stage door with my latest item of clothing my father had bought me which was a sheepskin coat with a fur collar. Byng came up to me and fingered the collar and said 'You're awfully well dressed for an electrician' and I said, 'I want to be an impresario!' He grabbed my hand and said 'Come with me!' He took me into his dressing room and I remember all the stage hands saying 'hang on!' He sat me down and said, 'Young man, all the producers I know apart from the Littler Brothers Prince and Emile, have gone bust. If you want to be an impresario get a business behind you! Do not listen to anybody else and you need to have money behind you. Even C. B. Cochran went bust but you have got to do it.' From that day we corresponded by letter and he did later offer to become a pantomime dame for me but gave up in the end and I don't know why. I think **Tom Arnold** had also offered him something at Manchester Palace Theatre, but he turned that down as well. He actually gave me some very good advice as synonymously; I was already starting to think about theatre management and beginning to get into the 'network'. I'd also met a chap called **Gilbert Harrison** who was the General Manager for Brian Rix, who also gave me some advice.

I actually advertised in 'The Stage' for a business manager vacancy, after I had met my life-long Australian friend Bill Pepper when I was only sixteen. He and I had been offered the rights to a play called 'Fanghorn'(10) which we liked but overnight Michael Codron, had bought these rights and staged it at the **Fortune Theatre** with Glenda Jackson and Penelope Keith. Marion Park and I saw it and thought it dull and so it seems did the public as it closed shortly afterwards.

Bill had to return to Australia because his mother was ill so my first attempt at management began to cool off. No one of course had given me any advice on what managing a production entailed or the finances involved and I had no idea how to go about it. Consequently, I thought; well I have just got to continue onwards regardless, having been buoyed up with all the artists I had met to date. I met a chap called Graham Stean who was Beatrix Potter's godson who had come down from the Lake District seeking to get into the theatre management business as well. Together we looked for a circle of people who could also be involved but again these aspirations went onto the back burner due to the lack of available schemes. In the meantime I resolved to just enjoy life!

As the Phoenix was dark again for a few months I was transferred to the Apollo Theatre in Shaftesbury Avenue and **'Spring and Port Wine'** by Bill Naughton (made into a film in 1970 with James Mason in the leading role). In the cast were Alfred Marks who was very good and the young John Alderton who was to go on to TV sitcoms such as **'Emergency Ward 10'** and **'Upstairs Downstairs'** and Jennifer Wilson playing one of the sisters, (who was later to work for me). I had been put in there however, because the Chief Electrician was going on a long holiday and they didn't trust the assistant electrician who was an old boy, as well as a 'bookies runner'.

Although I had to tell them that I had never worked on their computer board before, the response was, 'don't worry, do a "full-up" (i.e. put all the lights on) if there is a problem. We are more worried that this guy might be out betting and not doing his job'.

However, he was there all the time and was very nice but I will always remember the night when he had loads of bank notes as he always had because of his sideline in betting. It is funny how names in show business keep coming back into one's own life, although I don't think this is unusual in this 'village' (i.e. the theatre world) we live in. Everybody knows everybody who is anybody and it soon gets around through various producers who not to employ!

There was one memorable night when during the very hot summer of 1967 at the Apollo, an American poked his head through the scene dock door which had been left open, to air the theatre during matinees. As quick as a flash this deputy electrician, the bookies runner, said to him, 'Do you want to buy it?' I stood there in absolute amazement as he was on the point of selling Prince Littler's theatre to this American and I really think he would have done it! **'Spring and Port Wine'** was produced by Michael Medwin under Memorial Productions and he was best known for his roles in **'Shoestring'** and the **'Army Game'**. A fascinating chap and I have recently noticed his name again through David Pugh Limited in London, a theatrical production company for which he is the chairman.

So I spent that summer and the run up to Christmas, not only working at the Apollo but they also had me down at Her Majesty's as well. I used to run errands at the Theatre Royal Drury Lane where incidentally Cameron Mackintosh was around and I found out from the manager that they had sacked him although he was still there all the time. However, I never bumped into him and I have never officially met him. When the landlords Gerald and Veronica Flint-Shipman took back the Phoenix, they had all the ornate light shades designed by Theodore Komisarjevsky thrown out and replaced by standard white Flambeau's which we all hated and wondered why they had done this. This theatre was Grade II listed so how did he get away with it? Incidentally, I kept them all and stored them at home and eventually through John Earl at the Theatres Trust presented them to Geoffrey Wren, General Manager of Maybox Theatres who owned the Phoenix in the late 1980s. I also mentioned that spare parts for these ornate shades could be obtained via Granada Theatres. Unfortunately, they never went back and I do not know what happened to them after that. Two interesting things then happened to me. One was that they re-engaged me to stay at the Phoenix for the first production that came in which was a play and Ray Cooney's first West End production as a producer. It was a comedy thriller called, 'In at the Death', then re-written as **'Murder by the Book'**, which I later toured as a producer of my own very first production. It had an interesting cast with Terrance Alexander, Julien Holloway who was Stanley Holloway's son, Jean Kent and Nigel Hawthorne, all splendid people. Ray Cooney used to talk to me on the way home because he lived in Epping, re-kindling my thoughts about being a producer. Secondly, at about that time I was called to the manager's office for Prince Littler who had still kept his manager there to help Flint Shipman out. This was a guy called Peter Cornelia and he said,' You've had a large income tax rebate Michael and you shouldn't have one. What is your actual age? So I told him that I had just become seventeen and his face dropped. He said we shouldn't be employing you until you are eighteen, although you can do the job as the electrician but we have got to sort this out. I don't know what actually happened about this except that the master carpenter at the Phoenix called Alex Simmons, was Prince Littler's personal carpenter. He had been a barge builder before joining Prince Littler prior to the Second World War and lived in the Peabody flats near the theatre in Drury Lane. He calmly said to me 'Are you looking for a job, Mike?' and I said 'I don't know, why?' He said, 'Well there is one at the London Coliseum and they want an assistant electrician as it is a cinema and I can get you it!' On later reflection, this was how they found me a job in the interim until I was eighteen. I had often dreamt about working at the London Coliseum because it was Sir Oswald Stoll's theatre. So I went to see the chief electrician, Eric Cridland, in June 1967 and he said 'You can have the job because if Alex Simmonds has recommended you so I have no problems. You will now be working for **'Cinerama'** and not Stoll Theatres but the job is basically maintenance and being around in case a bulb goes out – all very simple work.' Of course, in the back of my mind was that when I got to eighteen I was going to go the Palladium as a technician. I therefore left the Phoenix and went to work for Cinerama, the big screen where **'The Bible'**, directed by John Houston, was playing.

This was quite something for me because I was an assistant electrician in the largest theatre in London and didn't I let everyone know it! The salary was thirteen pounds and eight shillings plus overtime, which meant I was getting more that I had earned at the Phoenix and I wanted to do this as part of the 'University of Life'. I met at the Coliseum some more fascinating people, having always had an attraction to this beautiful building which was named after the famous Coliseum in Rome and has been reportedly haunted by one ghost along with a host of soldiers. **(Chapter 6 - Some Theatre Phantoms)**

During my time there they embarked upon clearing out some of the under-stage store rooms and when Prince Littler came to supervise the throwing away of old records and memorabilia, I obtained his permission to keep some artefacts including pictures, which I still possess. Eric Cridland, who had engaged me not only knew the founders of Strand Electric, Earnshaw, but he'd worked for the previous company called 'Digby's'. **(11)** He would never start the day without finishing all the questions in the Daily Telegraph crossword and would always leave his pipe around the building, sometimes lit and why the theatre never went up in flames I don't know. Eric was a devout Catholic who sadly couldn't have children so he and his wife adopted twins. He was a very kind man who supported me when one day the manager caught me going out to tea early with Tom Arnold's secretary, Jackie. He actually said to the manager, 'Well, Michael always finishes the work I leave him' (not that he ever left me any work). It was through Jackie that I used to get free seats to a lot of shows. We used to go to the matinees and if night duties were off, which they sometimes were, we could go to the evening shows as well. I went to the opening nights of **'Sweet Charity'** and the **'Four Musketeers'** starring Harry Secombe at the Drury Lane, so I was really having a good time, which was a marvellous education for a seventeen-year-old. I also met Gerty Crocker at the Coliseum who was the then Catering Manager for Cinerama, but in the past a very old employee of Sam Harbour, the late General Manager of the Coliseum. She said one night that I reminded her of someone from her past, probably because I was a little shy and often spoke with monosyllabic answers. I said it was probably Sir Oswald as we shared the same birthday date! She did not give an answer but after that she was always respectful to me. However, all that was to end because they were announcing that Cinerama were giving up the lease of the Coliseum, as English National Opera (Sadler's Wells ENO) were thinking of taking it on. Raymond Lane the manager said to me 'Well you won't qualify for redundancy because you haven't done a year but I'll see if I can get you a job with Sadler's Wells. My friend Graham Stean had come back into my life as we had got the rights to a musical based upon **'Little Lord Fauntleroy'** (published in 1885 by Frances Hodgson Burnett) and adapted by David Williams who lived in Ramsgate. I did not know what I was letting myself into but I said to Raymond Lane, 'could we lease the Coliseum'? What was so ironical was that Raymond Lane was a devout Mason who knew Michael Friend whom, at that time I didn't know, but who was later to become another life-long friend of mine.

Raymond Lane said, 'Well if you want to be a producer Michael, I'll introduce you to people at Cranbourn Mansions.' This led me to Prince Littler's right hand man, Toby Rowland, who interviewed me but it didn't bare any fruit, also they did not want any electricians at Sadler's Wells because they were bringing in their own people. This meant that it was quite clear that I was going to be made redundant. In my mind was the question, could go to the Palladium if a job was still available or embark on some other journey in life? One of the projectionists at the Coliseum facing a similar question said, 'Well, I'm going back to my old cinema circuit to work as a projectionist and they also run theatres. Why don't you try and get management experience through one of these circuits?'

As Graham Stean's cousin had been head of light entertainment for **Granada** and Sidney Bernstein of Granada had built the Phoenix I thought that I should apply to Granada. They were the best of the small circuits and were theatres not cinemas, but they would not take me on until I was twenty-one. **The Odeon** circuit gave the same answer. The Coliseum projectionist then said, 'Well, I am going back to the ABC at Harrow, why don't you apply to ABC?' So I wrote to **ABC Cinemas** and I got a reply from their Establishment Officer in April 1968 about two months before we all were to leave the Coliseum. It was from the office of the Chief Executive of ABC who had sent my letter to the District Manager's Office for East London and I was offered an appointment to meet a chap called Lionel Johnson, at ABC 803 High Road Leyton. I remember him saying to me, 'You have good experience in theatre so at eighteen we can take you on as an Apprentice Trainee Theatre Manager. Did you fail any G.C.E's?' I said, 'No not one and I also managed to get the London Arithmetic Exam.' 'Oh splendid,' he said, 'just the sort of education for management. We can take you on but not at the salary you are currently on.' There were two things here, for I had not sat any G.C.E's, but this was my attempt to give the correct response. I think they were pleased to get a member of staff with some experience, but for low money as mine went down to eleven pounds per week from nineteen in the West End. The irony of all this is that I myself one day I would be Lionel Johnson's boss.

My employment with ABC commenced in May 1968 at the **ABC cinema 95 Mile End Road E1,** not far from Stepney Green Tube Station, having had only one week's holiday on leaving the Coliseum. This cinema on the site of the original **'Eagle Tavern'** had had a dancing platform in the grounds and was later known as **'Lusby's Summer and Winter Garden'**. The larger Paragon Music Hall of Varieties was rebuilt by Frank Matcham in 1885, later to become the **Empire** and by 1912 the Mile End Music Hall. By 1923 it was rebuilt by W R Glen as a modern cinema called **'The Regal'** and then 1939, it was taken over by the **ABC.**

In 1986 it became the Coronet after a series of closures and a period of uncertainty and in 1999, it was refurbished and re-opened as the **Genesis** Cinema which it remains to this day. It has recently been described as a beautiful independent cinema a short distance from Stepney Green station with a small screen with comfortable red sofas, cushions and warm blankets! **(12)**

The manager here was Norman Sharp, who became another father figure to me. He sat me down on the first day and said, 'I am going to teach you how the money comes in before I teach you how to spend it and if you remember this, then you will not go wrong in life.' He also taught me religiously the box office, the sales operations, sales checks, cleaning toilets, handling the queues, in those days consisting of a lot of multi-ethnic patrons and in six weeks, I had the most comprehensively-based training you could have wished for which was just as well. The later part of this training was to be at the ABC Leyton, which originally opened in July 1938 as the 'Ritz Cinema' with Joe E. Brown in **'Fit for a King'** and Frederick March in **'The Buccaneer'**.

The narrow external façade hid the enormity of a 1,532-seat auditorium as well as the 886 Circle and it was renamed ABC in October 1962. However, was later converted into office space with the front area occupied by Ladbrokes, the betting shop.

ABC Leyton

From here I was to transfer to the other side of London, as my father had been appointed Head Master at Herschel High School, Slough Buckinghamshire. **(13)** I was transferred on 10th June 1968 to the Regal Uxbridge where I was to work with a manager who seemed to me to prefer the pub to the theatre. I was literally thrown in at the deep end with limited experience to run the place by myself at times. This well-known Regal Uxbridge opened in 1931 and was built for A.E. Abrahams who operated Regal Cinemas at Marble Arch, West Norwood and Edmonton. (All now demolished.) **(14)**

The following pictures by courtesy of **'Creative Commons' license** (HYPERLINK "https://wiki.creative/"https://wiki.creative commons.org).

This cinema manager however was a great bloke who came from Kent and although I was still a trainee, within six months I had to go out on relief as they were often calling on me to help staff at other theatres as well, due to a management shortage. I even found myself going frequently to The Broadway at Hammersmith, which mainly featured off-circuit films. As a consequence of all this I was made up to an assistant manager in record time from the lowest grade D. Furthermore, because the managers I was relieving sent in quite nice reports to the District Manager, I was promoted to a Grade A Cinema Manager in July 1969. This District Manager said, 'As you doubtless know this will bring you an increase of one pound per week in your salary to seventeen pounds and ten shillings plus sales commission (which then was very good) and I am sure that this show of confidence in you will encourage you to carry on with the good work!' However, now at the age of nineteen I was over working again because we were operating on five twelve hour days per week, with little time off on the other two days and I took no holidays either. Being the only assistant manager with advance box office experience in that part of London I was shared around other cinemas and was getting somewhat tired. One morning having had no rest for a long period I collapsed with the runs and general tiredness and was off for a few days! Consequently, I began to think whether there might be any other job less stressful that I could do in the cinema circuit, as I had learnt the basic jobs all of which had contributed to my overall initiation into cinema management. Looking even further ahead, it was to be my past theatre experience that was to be very handy with the big release of **'Dr Zhivago'.**

From on the Doors to Advanced Booking

For the film **'Dr Zhivago'** ABC decided to go for booking in advance as opposed to the customary cash on the door, which was a precedent. I was the only theatre man on the circuit of North East London who knew about undertaking advance bookings. Consequently, I was somewhat over-used and I collapsed one day at home and a visit to the doctor meant a course of Valium to calm me down. It then occurred to me that if I could get a job at Head Office in film bookings or as an accountant or controller it might ease the work-load. Getting fed up with not getting anywhere with this request, on 11th March 1970 I wrote to Bernard Delfont who was the then Chairman and Chief Executive. He did reply to my letter, although he was unable to see me straight away and said he would be happy to chat to me and perhaps I could ring his secretary. In the end his secretary suggested I should write another letter to Mr Delfont because he was in or out of the country. On 13th March I had this lovely reply from him saying, 'Thank you for your letter. At the moment there are not any vacancies but if anything becomes available, I will contact you.' On this same day March 13th, I got a letter inviting me to be the 'Sales Co-ordinator in the Theatre Sales Department' at Head Office. I never smelt a rat but I thought that something must have happened to prompt this.

On meeting the Head of Theatre Sales, he said, 'I want you for the job and you will take on eighty cinemas and be required to go around and make sure that the sales operations are right!' I always thought that this was due to Bernie Delfont because he was always a good boy. So I had gone from being an assistant manager Grade A to the Head Office in March 1970 at the tender age of twenty. I stayed there until April 1971 and I was immediately plunged into the re-building programme, to convert old cinemas from single screens to twins and triples. I made a name for myself, when they re-opened the old Saville Theatre in Shaftesbury Avenue, where I worked over Christmas. In those days, cinemas in the West-End were there for showing new films, although the ABC was determined to let people know that we were there for in-house merchandising as well. I was put into the ABC 1 and 2 Shaftesbury Avenue in order to increase these sales which were not doing at all well. In my first week these sales increased and in the second week we hit the national average and the third week, we went above it. I got a pat on the back from everyone including commendation letters from Bernard Delfont. In truth these sales increases could be attributed to dating most of the sales girls! We all got very friendly which was my management style and I said, 'Look, come on, we've got to increase these sales!' They were kind of working for me rather than for ABC, which worked, because all sales apart from ice creams went up. I met a cockney girl who swore like a trooper whom I kept in touch with for some years and her name was Lynn. However, I was now to encounter some problems due to the company decision to remove the sales commission incentive for selling ice creams and other merchandise. Instead, managers would gain commission based on the increase in overall theatre takings. In short, the company had decided to give cinema managers a better basic salary, thereby reducing any incentive to employ more sales personnel to sell more confectionery and ice creams and consequently, they just sat in their offices unconcerned at all with the in-house sales.

Some Further Reflections on my Formative Years, of People and Situations

With hindsight I did not have a plan because situations and events just happened, although I entered into every opportunity on the basis of gaining experience and having the confidence to do whatever was required. With the ABC there were theatres such as at Southend-on-Sea where, under the floor, was the old Empire Theatre. The big Cardiff and Plymouth ABC's were pop-show venues. I became a major asset as the only chap from the theatre world, with knowledge of operating advance booking systems. When I went down to the West Country what would they be showing but **'Doctor Zhivago'**, for which everyone was on advance bookings. My official schedule was to undertake a theatre sales survey, but the managers having found out that I had this previous experience would ask me, 'Can you help me with the daily return for advanced bookings and also the operation of the advanced box office?' Doctor Zhivago I know backwards and I think is a beautiful film.

I will always remember the interval because we used to get all the ice cream girls ready and when he says 'that is Strelnikoff' when the train goes off in the distance. That is the point when I used to say 'Go!' and we used to get the ice cream girls down and just flog the ices at 1/6d per tub systematically. On reflection I feel that those were wonderful days for me.

Theatre management depends crucially upon having trust in your staff through knowing their work, or from the recommendations of others whose opinions could be trusted and respected, much of which is relayed by word of mouth. Again, any experience was learned through doing it. Say as an actor going through the repertory system having had a brief training at a drama school although for some not for all. Many are simply flung in at the deep-end at rep as experienced by Michael Friend who went to RADA as a designer and ended up working at the Guildford Rep. This he still talks about as well as when he employed a young Alan Ayckbourn. Such experience has been suggested as the best way of learning but it is essentially relationship focussed and nurtured, which is important in any field but especially in the theatre as a people industry. It involves getting into the business and networking, as well as going out and socialising with one's peers and gaining as well from their and the experiences of others.

One unexpected hair-raising challenge was that at the Regal Uxbridge on the final night of Dr. Zhivago we had a three-hour power cut and the house had been pre-sold out! After half an hour the lights, having not returned except for one phase on the secondary lighting and the Compton organ, we had to invite people to be given a refund on their tickets. We telephoned Head Office via the District Office as to what to do, as this had never happened before because cinemas then did not normally sell advance tickets. We quickly sold off the ice creams as the fridges were down and as fast as the loot came in, out went the refunds. Lights came back on at 9.45 ish and we held a midnight matinee for all those who had stayed patiently in the gloom. I cannot remember how we cashed up but absolutely no one from Head Office or District level gave any help with this dilemma and literally did a bunk on this crisis! What had been learned was from going through with this experience was just get on with it.

At a more personal level, whilst at the ABC Uxbridge through the local bank, I met a Peter and Teresa Johnson, who had just become engaged and who would later ask me to become Godfather to their first son James. Peter later worked for British Airways as his father was the company secretary and he arranged to conduct me on a private tour around Concorde the supersonic airliner, which was a wonderful experience, although I have to say that I found this highly topical plane to be claustrophobic! We kept a friendship up for some years and they came to my marriage to Terrie as well as being 'Angels' on my first theatre production. This is an example of contacts, through work experience becoming friends for they were a lovely couple. What is sad is that we somehow eventually lost contact.

Eve Griffiths – A Memorable and Important Friend

On my first day at the Regal Uxbridge the manager said, 'You'll meet tonight a lady who was in the theatre and is our evening cashier, Eva Griffiths' (who preferred to be known as Eve). I always remember going downstairs and there was this little short Welsh lady and that was it. I don't know whether it was love or what but we got on so well although there was a fifty-year age difference between us. She was actually like a grandmother to me, but I called her my 'Sugar Mummy' which was completely platonic. We had a mutual love of the theatre and she passed over to me the programmes of the Royal Court Liverpool, and the re-building of the Midland Adelphi Hotel in Liverpool and various letters from people like Edgar Lustgarten (1907–1978), a noted crime writer and a graduate of St John's College Oxford. She also taught me the delights of life like brandies and Babycham and Havana cigars. Although I don't know whether she saw me as the man she never married, a Mr James Hare, who ran the Bangor Theatre (6) When I put on one of my tours and was at Bangor in North Wales, for a story I asked the local papers whether anyone could remember Eva and it was amazing what was found. One old boy said, 'I thought that there was something going on between this lady and the manager of the theatre!' Eve had just died when I did this story. In 1947 she was at Denham Studios as head of 'Preview Theatres', inspecting every print after a film had been made to make sure that there were no flaws in it. Actually, when colour films first appeared, she had a nervous breakdown because of all the spots on the screen. She acted as my mentor and if I had any problems with girlfriends she would offer her advice.**Error! Bookmark not defined.**

Eve Griffiths in the grounds of Uppark House South Harting Petersfield W Sussex (15)

Eve was an absolutely lovely lady and when she died I was the executor of her will. What little of her finances that were left went to a woman who seemed to just want her money. With the help of Eve's old friends, we got enough together for her gravestone, which her sole beneficiary did not pay anything towards. We had the inscription, **'This headstone is donated by the friends of the little lady with the big heart!'** The vicar questioned why I had this inscription and after the funeral director told him the circumstances, he allowed it. I have visited this grave regularly and have maintained the insurance on it. My co-executor was the secretary for the Chichester Festival Theatre.

Through her association, especially with Chichester, has convinced me of the importance of establishing good and lasting relationships. I had known Eve during her last twenty years and it could be said that through her and people like her, whom I have met and known, my own life has been enriched!

References

(1) Widowers Houses by George Bernard Shaw
This was Shaw's first play and staged at the Royalty Theatre on 9th December 1892. It was performed by a subscription club 'Independent Theatre Society', to escape the Lord Chamberlain's censorship. It was originally written in 1885 in collaboration with a William Archer but there was disagreement between the two. Shaw re-organised it and added a third act. This is one of three plays which Shaw published as 'Plays Unpleasant' in 1898 because it was not intended to entertain, which was the expectation of a Victorian audience, but to raise awareness of social problems and condemn exploitation of the laboring class by the unproductive rich. Plays also in this genre are 'The Philanderer' and 'Mrs. Warren's Profession'.
(Taken from Wikipedia -This previous text is available under the HYPERLINK https://en.wikipedia.org/wiki/Wikipedia:Text_of_Creative_Commons_Attribution-ShareAlike_3.0_Unported_License "https://www.wikimediafoundation.org/"Wikimedia Foundation, Inc., a non-profit organization).

(2) Phyllida Law
Phyllida Law was born in 1932 in Glasgow and was married to actor Eric Thompson from 1957 until his death in 1982. Their daughters, Emma and Sophie Thompson were both actresses. Phyllida Law has appeared in many documentaries and interviews concerning her late husband's work on 'The Magic Roundabout' and has worked extensively in television and films.

(3) Theatre Royal Stratford East
The original building was designed by a James George Buckle and opened on 17th December 1884 being owned by an actor manager Charles Dillon, who sold it in 1886 to Albert O'Leary Fredericks, his sister's brother-in-law and one of the original backers. Fredericks added side extensions in 1887 and in 1891 enlarged the stage. In 1902, the architect Frank Matcham (who also designed the Hackney and Finsbury Park Empires) made minor improvements to the entrance and foyer. The Fredericks family managed this theatre until 1932, although it only opened on an irregular basis from 1926, due to financial difficulties post-First World War. Fred Fredericks is said to haunt this theatre (see Chapter 6).

4. Theatre Workshop
This was a touring company who presented a Christmas pantomime in 1950 and returned in 1953, as 'Theatre Workshop,' with artistic director Joan Littlewood. The construction of the Stratford Shopping Centre put this theatre under threat in the 1970s, but it was saved due to a public campaign through English Heritage and in addition it had been designated as a Grade II listing. The front of house was refurbished in 1984 and in 2001, as a result of a successful Lottery Fund Bid. A re-development of the back-stage area was also undertaken as part of the Stratford Cultural Quarter.

(5) Akinwande Oluwole "Wole" Soyinka was born in July and became notable as a playwright and poet by winning the Nobel Peace Prize for Literature in 1986 and the first black African to be so honoured. He studied in Nigeria before working at the Royal Court Theatre London, writing plays performed in theatres and on radio in both countries. He was also a campaigner for Nigerian independence from Great Britain. He later lived mainly in the United States and was a professor first at Cornell University and then Emory University Atlanta, where in 1996 he was appointed as Robert W Woodruff, Professor of the Arts.

(6) Something Nasty in the Woodshed is based on an unforgettable character known as Great Aunt Aida from 'Cold Comfort Farm' which is a comic novel by Stella Gibbons published in 1932. Great Aunt Aida has been reclining in bed on four meal trays per day. Cold Comfort Farm is regarded as a parody of the tragic Gothic novels by Mary Webb and D.H. Lawrence. It was adapted into a John Schlesinger film in 1995(author and songs not listed in Ovtur a theatre database).

(7) Prince Littler he was the eldest son of five children born to Jules Richeux a cigar importer and his wife Agnes May. Blanche was his elder sister. Richeux leased the Ramsgate Victoria Pavilion in 1906 whilst Alice leased the Artillery Theatre Woolwich. After Jules Richeux's death in 1911 Agnes re-married Frank Rolison Littler in 1914 and adopted all five children. With Blanche his younger sister he began assembling small companies for tours of the provinces in 1927 and became a theatre owner in 1931 having bought two theatres in Leicester. He married a widow professionally known as the actress and singer Norah Delaney who also performed in Music Hall as Marie Lloyd. His first productions in London were pantomimes at Drury Lane. Then Ivor Novello's **'Glamorous Night** (1936) **'Brigadoon'** (1950), **'Carousel'** (1951), **'Guys and Dolls'** (1953), **'Can-Can'** (1954) **'The Black and White Minstrel Show'** and (1966) **'Fiddler on the Roof'**. Littler was Managing Director of three major theatre groups and Chairman of Moss Empire.

(8) Hugh known as Binkie Beamont
Sir Peter Saunders in his book **'Mousetrap Man',** published in 1972, states that Binkie Beaumont and John Perry of the H.M. Tennent company raised the state of British Theatre after 1947 to new heights, having sometimes ten or twelve shows at a time playing in the West End. No one presented plays and musicals as well as Beaumont did and the greatest authors and stars flocked to him. He could find work for his leading actors due to his first claim on productions. This had been born largely through a clever manipulation of the 'Entertainment Tax,' which by then had grown to a penal 38% of theatre takings (not profits). This tax was introduced during the First World War in 1916, as a temporary emergency measure. The grounds were that if a theatrical producer loved the theatre sufficiently to take no profit, he would receive some government support against a loss. After the Second World War, a non-profit making company would gain total exemption from this tax if they could demonstrate that they were doing works which had an educational or cultural element. In addition to this, allowing for

producers' expenses at £40 per week, as well as other legitimate expenses being withdrawn from the takings. With a non-profits company no one would be interested in investing in a venture which could at best break even and at worst make a loss. The government therefore increased the insurance against making any loss, with the proviso that the aims of the company should still be cultural and educational. This did not bar putting on other productions such as bedroom farces and thrillers. If playing for £3,000 revenue per week, an additional insurance against loss could be obtained at £1,200. Binkie Beaumont exploited this situation to become in the longer term a London West End dictator. He was not allowed to pay his stars excessive rates and he might have five productions on at the same time. Other companies such as the Mask Theatre run by Thane Parker tried to do the same but had had no ambition to dominate the market. Consequently, here was a situation in which Binkie had first call on all the best stars and plays which were sent to him before anyone else. Stars even turned down higher salaries elsewhere in order to hang round him in the notion that they would be 'looked after' in a general way (perhaps gain continuous employment opportunities?). Consequently, they could afford to take lesser terms than commercial managements. Even a play agent would not wish to offend Binkie Beaumont by offering a work to another producer with the result that seldom did productions other than his get into the Shaftesbury Avenue theatres in the late forties and early fifties, including Drury Lane the Haymarket and Her Majesty's.

There were even cases when an unpopular production might be keeping the theatre warm for a following one to be introduced? At one time his company H.M. Tennent and a rival Linnet and Dunfee, had 'tied up' fifteen West End theatres between them. The Member of Parliament for Birmingham Aston, Woodrow Wyatt, was approached with a view to bringing a bill before parliament to prevent this continued monopoly by one man both in the West End and who had a growing influence also in the provinces. A situation regarded as dangerous where producers who died were not being replaced. The major limitation was that anyone including an international star that would be in support of this bill wished to be anonymous, for fear that they would be barred from further acting or directing roles. After extensive research Woodrow Wyatt found that Beaumont had been extremely honourable and had raised the professional standard of theatre to a new level, but who had exploited the exemption of entertainment duty in order to build up a great theatrical empire. Another astonishing revelation was that Tennant Productions were registered as a charitable trust, as well as a theatre producing company and paying no income tax at all. A factor which had prevented other commercial companies from getting into the best theatres in London, as well as obtaining first rate actors. However, professionals in the theatrical world who supported a parliamentary bill wished to retain anonymity. However, in 1954 a bill brought before parliament to remove these abuses, failed to reach the statute book. Furthermore, after further lobbying, a conservative budget of Peter Thorneycroft in 1957 contained a statement that the Entertainment Tax on theatre revenues was unfair as it was not based upon profits. That it would be withdrawn completely in 1958.

(9) Annette Mills and 'Muffin the Mule'
She was known for working with a famous puppet created by a Punch and Judy maker, Fred Tickner in 1934 called 'Muffin the Mule'. Anne Hogarth, who had purchased the puppet for fifteen shillings (75p) from the creator, manipulated it whilst Annette Mills sang and played the piano. It was broadcast on BBC Children's Television between 1946 and 1952.

(10) Legendarium by J R Tolkien was a forest located in the fictional world of 'middle earth'. The home of tree shepherds or 'Ents', the oldest known as 'Treebeard'. The Forest of Fanghorn provided an important role in *'The Lord of the Rings'* novel.

(11) Strand Electric
This is the original name for a company created by two London theatre technicians, Arthur Earnshaw and Philip Sheridan in 1914. In 1968 this company was purchased by The Rank Film Corporation becoming 'Rank Strand'. Then in 1969 Rank acquired Century Lighting founded in New York in 1929. In 1986 bought an Italian based manufacturer of TV and Film lighting. In 1976, Rank acquired Stagesound Ltd from Theatre Projects and created Rank Strand Sound. Then in 1986 Rank Strand bought Quartzcolor, an Italian based manufacturer of TV & Film Lighting. In 1990 Strand Lighting became the first company and only North American Company to gain ISO9000 quality certification. In the late 1990s the company was bought by Rank then in 2006 it was acquired by the Genlyte Group a US company. Since then it has been acquired by Royal Philips Lighting, under which still operates today as a separate independent company within it, continuing as a lead name in stage, television, motion pictures and architectural lighting services. (Wikipedia)

(12) Sir William Herschel (1738–1822) was a Hanoverian British Astronomer and a composer of 24 symphonies and many concertos. He also discovered the planet Uranus on 13th March 1771, was knighted by George III and became Astronomer Royal and a Fellow of the Royal Society (FRS). This high school in Slough bears his name.

(13) Mile End Music Hall-The new Empire Cinema was designed by ABC's chief architect, William R. Glen F.R.I.A.S and opened on the 12th of June 1939 with the films **'Burn 'Em Up O'Connor'** and **'Persons in Hiding'**. The Cinema was designed in the Art Deco style and was equipped with a small stage and two dressing rooms but film has dominated its programming ever since. In 1973 the Cinema was tripled and the façade was re-clad. Cannon Cinemas bought the building in 1986 and renamed it Cannon but soon after it was bought by Coronet Cinemas and renamed Coronet in October 1986. Three years later the Cinema was closed and it then stood derelict for more than ten years, being damaged by vandals and suffering a small fire in the process. According to the 'Cinema Treasures Website' this building was restored by a local Tyrone Walker-Hebborn, who spent £3 million and added another two screens. This cinema re-opened on 5th of May 1999 with the film 'True Crime'. Barbara Windsor had the honour of opening this **Genesis** Cinema that still remains in this form today. **(Ref: Cinema Treasures Website)**

14) Regal Cinema Uxbridge – Designed by E. Norman Bailey. Externally it had motifs depicting ancient Egypt and internally some amazing art deco. Today it is regarded as one of the most important original cinema buildings in London. It first opened on Boxing Day in 1931 with the film 'Reaching for the Moon', staring Douglas Fairbanks Sr. and Bebe Daniels. The internal façade contained tiled Egyptian motifs and in front to the left of the stage was a Compton Organ, still I situ today in a glass case. There was a café as well as a ballroom. It 1935 it came under the management of 'Union Cinemas' and from 1937 Associated British Cinemas (ABC). Operating as a cinema until 1977 it was then graded as a Grade II listed building, but was empty until May 1984. The stage area had been bricked in and separated from the auditorium becoming a gymnasium and health club. In 2007 renewal took place once more as the 'Liquid Envy Nightclub' a 'Regal Nightclub', the organ being retained but not functioning.

(15) Uppark House South Harting Petersfield W.Sussex - Now owned by the National Trust this house was built for Sir William Ford Grey who was the first Earl of Tankerville. It has beautiful views of the South Downs and English Channel. The upper floor was destroyed by fire in 1991 and it was later restored to its former glory in the largest £20 million-pound project undertaken by the National Trust. Eve Griffiths is pictured in the grounds of this house before the fire. Most of the contents of the house including antique furniture and paintings were saved from this fire.

Chapter 3 – Theatres and Cinemas Require Entrepreneurship as well as Business Acumen

In March 1970, now as a sales co-ordinator at ABC Head Office, I was to discover first hand some of the personality characteristics of 'key staff', some of whom I had met earlier on. To put it bluntly, I found most of them to be quite useless as they just could not run a theatre, although they actually dared to tell the theatre managers how to! To me they were like little 'Hitler's,' who had gained a position of power but were unable to do the job themselves. Equally, some whom I had met in the arts authorities could not run a theatre either and were trying to tell me how to, which was so frustrating. Sadly, in my experience this is endemic in British society where, if you are a failure, say as a member of the council, you are not sacked but moved to another job. Intuitively I feel that this is wrong because if you cannot perform the role yourself then you ought to go.

Bernard Delfont was now running ABC as an acquisition of EMI which seemed curious. Was this acquisition made due to ABC's immense property holdings and liquid assets? In reality EMI was now failing as a company, largely due to the gradual loss of the Beatles vast income from their releases, as well as the profits and royalties from their songs. The 'hay days' for EMI (who originated from HMV) having now gone, meant that other funding sources had to be found for research and development, for instance on medical projects. So EMI bought out 25% of the ABC circuit controlled by Warner Brothers. This initiative had stemmed from 'The Monopolies Commission Report' in November 1968, by the Harold Wilson government. At that time Warner Brothers owned twenty-five percent of the major British cinema circuit which was unacceptable because this report had stipulated overall control must be by a British company. The response to this was that EMI bought Warner Brothers twenty five percent and mounted a takeover bid for ABC cinemas, which they won. Bernard Delfont had lots of good policies for modernising the circuit which were long overdue. Through gaining control of ABC, it was revealed in the press that its founder John Maxwell, had created a property company with a Robert Clark, who was another ABC Director. In addition to this he also owned the 'Stock Loan & Conversion Trust', which was ex-'Great Central Railway' and another property concern. This meant that between them they actually owned most of the freeholds of the ABC cinemas, which in turn they had leased back to the ABC company. Apart from operating 360 cinemas, over the years ABC had turned some into bingo halls or leased them out to smaller operators. At a rough estimate this might have involved over 200 units on which they had kept the freeholds, which was all perfectly legal!

Of the three hundred and sixty live cinemas ABC had throughout the country I was in charge of the East Anglia circuit from Norwich, right down through London to Cornwall; in all, about a third of the entire operation. A lot of these cinemas were converted theatres which absolutely fascinated me because when the on-site administrative work and monitoring the theatre sales had been completed, I was then free to view and admire an original old theatre; such as the Old Empire, Southend-on-Sea, Essex as well as the Marina Theatre in Lowestoft, Suffolk.

Empire, Southend-on-Sea, Essex from a 1905 postcard

The Empire is an historic theatre originally a hall converted by Frederick Marlow in 1892 but burnt down in 1895 which he rebuilt into a much larger theatre that included electric lighting. **(1)**

Lowestoft Marina Theatre - Theatres' Trust Archives

Auditorium of the Marina Theatre – Also Theatres' Trust Archives

Saville Theatre (Theatres Trust Picture)

On the operational side I was able to learn from other managers how they ran their particular units. Some were very good and could have run the whole circuit themselves, which was a verification why the management had stipulated that if you were a grade A Manager you should stay at the coalface. Significantly, at this time Bernie Delfont was for speeding up the programme of converting old pre-war cinemas from a single screen into twin cinemas and even multiplexes. He was often personally involved in re-opening a lot of these which also stimulated my interest. Perhaps the best example was the old **Saville Theatre (2)** in Shaftesbury Avenue, London that Delfont had bought and now controlled which became the **'ABC Shaftesbury Avenue,'** proving to be another valuable experience for me. Previously it had been amongst his companies, bought and sold allegedly to avoid tax. However, he had sold it to the ABC circuit enabling it to be their first West End cinema. From the start it was to prove a success whilst most others weren't, as cinema circuits in London at that time were primarily to preview films rather than promote ticket sales. By contrast ABC was determined to act as a showcase for films as well as the in-house merchandising of ice creams and confectionery.

ABC Shaftesbury Avenue

Playing at the Saville was the 1970s film **'There's a Girl in My Soup'**, (3) featuring Peter Sellars which I saw many times and to this day, still laugh at. In house sales as a sideline were well illustrated by the old 'ABC Number One' which had a rear auditorium sales kiosk, with a non-silent shutter, similar to that in a jeweller's shop. It was never used because every time it was opened it sounded like an avalanche of tea trolleys which would wake the audience up. However, over a three-week period I took the sales above the national average and letters of commendation flowed in. What I didn't tell them was that I was dating all the girls so they were improving the sales for me, rather than for the company! I also discovered that it was important to have an active manager and not one with overall responsibility for just everything. I suggested a manager for in-house theatre sales, which of course was only viable if the sales potential was high, in addition to another manager for theatre administration. Unsurprisingly, when the sales turnover turned to 'too good' they pulled me out. I remember one accolade letter to Bernie Delfont which I saw but never was allowed to have, saying that thanks to Mr Michael Wheatley-Ward, we had pushed the theatre sales up. This was to prove to be a valuable example for the circuit as a whole and everyone higher than me was getting patted on the back for my work. I suppose this was nothing unusual and was probably to keep me in my place. Of course, apart from in-house sales it was vitally important to control costs as well in order to improve the overall profitability.

However, at a personal level I was over-doing it again and started to consider how I might get back into theatre or theatre buildings. I was now twenty and Graham Stean, whom I first met whilst working at the Phoenix Theatre said to me one day, 'I need someone to run my office in Wardour Street. You want to get back into the theatre and if I let you have free use of this office, that will help you set up your own production company!' Incidentally, Graham had been brought up in the Lake District in the village of Sawrey, his father having died, his mother re-married and Beatrix Potter was his godmother. My arduous schedule at this time was going away on a Monday morning and back on a Friday night and during the week I could be in an hotel in Cheltenham, Penzance, Dover, Norwich, in fact anywhere on the circuit. Additionally, I would help the Regal Cinema Uxbridge manager who had taken over from me when I left, with his book work on a Saturday night. Consequently, I was getting just Sunday off after travelling through the week and not taking the rest, which I should have done and I could see myself burning out. My social life was just in the theatre and cinema world and I didn't really have many friends other than Marion Park the actress, as my life at that time was primarily liaising with other managers. I could sometimes go to a local theatre during the week at the various places in which I was staying and especially when I was in London. During this period, I still lived with Mum and Dad as a base and sometimes met with old school friends as well as new friends I made who were around the circuit. For example, in Bristol I met what would become another life-long friend Arthur Brown, who ran a theatre there who sadly has recently died of leukaemia. Some of these management friends actually became personal friends including Graham Stean, who was gay and got the first gay cinema club going, as well as taking over an active secretarial bureau in a Wardour Street office. When at a later stage he said would I like to help operate this I said okay and stuck it for six months, although I had no income other than from weekend work from old ABC cinema manager contacts.

An Opportunity for a Theatre Production Company?

Then we came to a 'watershed,' because Graham Stean wanted this first gay cinema in London to be in a preview theatre, but it was right under Nat Cohen's offices in Wardour Street. This was after the passing of the Sexual Offences Act 1967 and the legalisation, within specific limits, of homosexual relationships. Nat Cohen didn't like the idea of a gay cinema and put a court injunction on it stopping it being opened. Graham came to me and said, 'Look Michael, I need someone to work with me who is basically straight. Would you like to get your theatre production company going at my offices?' This was to be 'Wardour Stage Productions' based at 132 Wardour Street. I often reflect back on this and come to the assumption that here was a period in my life when nothing would seem to gel and I concluded that, 'What will be will be!'(3) Doors open and close for a reason and this one had remained closed because nothing took off, although in itself it proved to be valuable training.

During this fallow period with nothing much happening I was gaining a different experience through trying to search for plays and visit literary agents. This would be part of my 'time invested' in gaining a different experience at the very least. I was not actually losing any money, since that would come later. Consequently, at the ABC I had reached a lull after charging around opening up theatres and cinemas, in addition to undertaking inspections. In reality though, I felt that I wanted to get back to being a producer as these inspections were purely on theatre sales administration and devoid of any artistic challenge. I had a special 'medal', a pass, and my job was to make sure that theatre managers had enough stock of merchandise to cover the next six weeks and that their turnover was good.

Furthermore, that the ice creams were presented properly and the kiosk was operated with sales maximisation as the main objective. I had nothing to do with structural operations or safety and fire regulations. Consequently, I was primarily an inspector for the sales department making sure that cinema managers were given credence for what they did well. To do all this I was travelling from Norwich to Falmouth and I had just started to get a car, an Austin 1100, which I used or went by train. A day was spent in each cinema and I had to fill out a report on my observations and from this, award the managers an overall performance grade standard. I remember going round the West Country – which was a very well run section of ABC and even meeting an old theatre manager at the ABC Cardiff whose secretary ran the office. He had staff parades which meant that they were all lined up in uniform and told where they were going to be and at what time they would be allocated a break, which was all very well regimented. I met other managers who used to let the staff cash up as they would just not do it. Of course, the one valuable thing that Norman Sharp had taught me was 'You keep your hands on the money otherwise it will go out of the door and you are still the one with the overall responsibility for it!' Norman Sharp was a wonderful manager whom I knew in his forties and kept in touch with. He was to turn up much later in my life at my home Chandos House in Ramsgate, on a couple of sticks accompanied by his wife Elma, just because he wanted to see me, after an interval of about ten years. He was like a second father to me and became an investor in one of my own shows. He was trained by the manager of the **ABC Plymouth** Bill Clark, who had trained another manager the same age as me called Arthur Brown, whom I had also met at Bristol. I recall that although those days at ABC travelling round the country were fascinating, time-wise I was scheduled in this function at Head Office for only just over a year.

My Very Own Venture – Wardour Stage Productions

Graham Stean and his cousin Phillis who was Head of Light Entertainment at Granada Theatres had started up this agency called 'Marks and Trevor'. Phillis, Graham Stean and I were on the list registered with Westminster Council at this first-floor office in Wardour Street. Graham also had a theatre in East London which was the first Gay Cinema Club, but he went bust because he was not that good with money. The question was, 'Would I work for him for nothing?' Of course, this was important as it gave me an opportunity to set up my own 'Theatre Productions', having had enough money saved for a year's living expenses. It enabled me to take the plunge and be actually licensed by Westminster Council as an agent, which was a job I actually hated. I had started Wardour Stage Productions in a premises with Graham but I found that I really could not get anywhere with it. People were coming to this office asking for money to do with the debts owed by the Gay Cinema Club and I had to say, 'I am sorry, but I am running **Wardour Stage Productions.'**

It was also extremely difficult to try to raise any money for my ventures as productions, since I did not actually know what was going on with Graham and Gay Cinema Projects due to my naivety at that time. Graham's cousin Phillis was a great lady, but even she fell out with him and sadly in the end he was destined to die of Aids, of which I was not to know. Years later on a visit to the Lake District with my wife Terrie, I wanted to go to see Beatrix Potter's home as she had been Graham's godmother. Psychic thoughts led me to the church where I just walked over and found his grave. I opened up a communication with his step mother who initially thought I was one of the many creditors after the estate but in fact I'd been a friend and I just wanted to know what had happened to him. She explained the situation and I was able to give a donation to place flowers on the grave in his memory. I admit that I had personally found Graham's enterprises to be a bit dodgy financially and my attempt to set up as an agent as well as a theatre producer, for reasons 'best known to mice and men', just did not click. This was probably due to my trying to run before I could walk which was another learned experience! On the other hand, I did meet the owner of Haslemere Estates who wanted to convert and modernise old buildings, which reinforced my interest in theatre history once again. We talked, discussed and approached the owners of several West-End theatres about buying them and incorporating office blocks above them, to enable their longer term viability and security. One site was the old Shaftesbury Theatre London where we considered building an office block above it to raise equity to restore the infrastructure of the theatre itself. Basically, this meant selling the 'air rights' as they do in America. We looked at all theatres and got close to buying the Globe now the Gielgud, the Queen's in Shaftesbury Avenue and the Strand Theatre, but none of this worked out. In the end all of these theatres went to Cameron Mackintosh and on reflection I realised that I had been entirely out of my league. During all this time I actually hadn't left the ABC as I had stayed on for a small income as a relief manager.

On the positive side I had been freed from the stress of having to go around a large section of cinemas from Suffolk to the South and South West and was instead enjoying life whilst just making ends meet. Coincidentally, ABC was off-loading surplus cinemas to smaller operators. As I knew some of these sites and I had met a Peter Prowting, a property developer and I felt that through him there might be some business opportunities. However, when it was discovered that I was part of ABC management any opportunities abruptly ended!

Then a further realisation occurred that I ought to try another attack at getting a business in a safer environment such as retail, which could act as a theatre business 'back-up,' as Douglas Byng had said. Although my full-time salary at the ABC Head Office had been about £35 per week at that time which was more than managers in general earned in those days, but of course, I had been doing a hell of a lot more work. As a single person it was a liveable salary and I was able to buy a car. However, as an alternative I decided that I would take a temporary job in a department store over the Christmas period as an experiment, whilst still working in ABC cinemas part-time. I went for an interview and they took me on at **'Suters of Slough'** which was the epitome of **'Are You Being Served,'** and a complete eye-opener. When they discovered that I had been a manager of a cinema and a theatre and having actually run them, I got quickly promoted and I went from 'boy's wear' to 'youth wear' to 'main men's wear' and I thought 'here we go again'. It was in my opinion, very badly run as a family business and as I was not learning a great deal so I changed jobs to a private tailor's in Uxbridge near the Regal cinema, which of course enabled me to still do the relief work as well. That is where I met Gordon Rippington who was a new manager who sat me down one day after about three or four weeks and said 'Well, we are both wasting our time here why don't we get our own shop going? You want to get a theatre and I'd like to get my own business,' so I said 'Well, that's a great idea, but how are we going to find the money? Let's first find the premises,' and we came upon this old shop in Slough High Street which was only on a temporary lease. We went to both our parents and I gave my father an insurance policy worth a thousand pounds which was due to be paid out within a year and on that he loaned me the cash.

He was a great man but would only do this on some security and 'Not for nothing, Michael!' Gordon did likewise with his mother so we had two thousand pounds in the bank. We both had a credit card and we went round our mates the manufacturers to see if they would loan us the stock to open up this shop, which they did. We re-fitted the shop ourselves with help from my mate Brian Winterbourne's dad who was a shop fitter and we then opened up. Within the first year we took fifty-five thousand pounds which absolutely amazed the bank. We only had a £2,500 overdraft on all the stock and we were both earning, which is probably equivalent to half a million these days. The stock was Van Heusen and Steegan suits, also DAKS, the whole lot. It was quite interesting for me having tried to be a theatre businessman for years and not financially getting anywhere. By contrast, on opening up in a standard retail shop I'm into a change for a new car as well as gaining a major increase in living standards. Also I continued to work part-time for ABC as well, although only because I wanted to keep my hand in.

All the managers that knew me were quite keen for me to be around because they didn't have a permanent relief manager. Even the ABC Maidenhead had to close for a period due to the lack of one, so this also became my other role as I took a day off from my shop. This meant that I never really left ABC and I became conscious that I could be overworking yet again. The first shop became a second shop and I was able to get my first house in Devon as a bolt-hole at Bampton, north of Tiverton, whilst also living with my parents in Buckinghamshire. Inevitably, because of the usual rent rises, we had to look around for replacement shops, because for some reason rents always went up faster than the turnover. We were offered the chance of buying the private Royal Tailors in Windsor, as we had written to Frank Radnor who owned the shop of that name down by the Theatre Royal Windsor, whom we heard was retiring. Ironically Radnor's was a military shop located at 39 Thames Street, selling military ties and badges which had also been under royal patronage because late George V1 went there as the Duke of York when Frank Radnor's father had been the tailor.

One Hundred Steps

We used to get quite a lot of royalty on private business including King Olaf of Norway, the Duke of Edinburgh, the Queen Mother's equerry and it was nice to think that although we were not actually under royal warrant, we were known to be under royal patronage. The business was situated right opposite the **'One Hundred Steps'** which was the private entrance to the Queen. The other shops we owned had to go in order to finance the purchase of this one, such as our second shop at Chertsey which was sold to buy Radnor's but the buyer did not pay rent and Sainsbury's rightly claimed it all back from us.

Nonetheless we did pay back rent and also sued our solicitors for wrong advice, which we won with full payment. We also worked with the House of Lords select committee on lease-hold reform. Just Gordon and I ran the shop together with a mail order facility. We expanded the business so much so that within the first year what we had paid for in business outlay we had recovered in sales. In those days before the big chains had started individual shops developed and thrived on their own individual personalities. My partner Gordon was brilliant at selling and he was a great comedian and we are still friends to this day. Between the two of us it was like a double-act on stage and it just worked. Our purchasing was also good but it gradually became evident that selling on the high streets was set to disappear. Although by anchoring ourselves in Windsor, which was a tourist town and by keeping our shop looking old fashioned, we used to trap the tourists. It got to the point in the end that probably 90% of our trade was from this source. Military lapel pins would sell to Japanese tourists like anything. You could not sell them the actual guards' regimental tie but you could these other accessories. So we kept that business which was going to close in 1984, for another twenty years, by adapting with the times and running it literally between us on a 'shoe-string'. We had bought it in 1984 but at that same time I was yearning to get back as a producer. It was one of those quirks of fate that I went to see **'Barnham'** starring Michael Crawford on the 19th January 1982, which was his fortieth birthday. I sat there, 'counting the house' as we call it and thinking I really ought to come back into theatre now that I am financially self-sufficient, although I did not know what the state of the theatre was actually like now and I knew only two producers from my youth, one was Michael Cordron, the other was Peter Saunders. **(4)** So I wrote to the now Sir Peter Saunders and he said 'Read my autobiography called the **'Mousetrap Man'** and if you still want to stay in the business come and see me.' So I did and I met the great man in his office at the Vaudeville Theatre out of mere curiosity but also because I wanted to get my hands on what they call 'the agreement between angels', in other words, investors and a producer, which he willingly gave me. I also asked him about literary agents where I could get plays from in those days.

Sir Peter Saunders Chairman and Managing Director, West End Theatre Managers Ltd: Theatre Investment Fund Ltd: Theatre Investment Finance Ltd with his wife Lady SAUNDERS (Katie Boyle) TV Presenter and former model. COMPULSORY CREDIT: Starstock/Photoshot Photo UIW 008326/B-01 (PRINTABLE INVOICE G800073/18) – Rights managed 5/4/20 (Image 01ASV6Z2-Rights managed 5/4/18

I said, 'I have lost my entire contacts do you mind if I keep in touch?' and he said, 'No, the phone is always there, I will help you out as long as you help other people out when you get to that point'. I have always remembered that, so any problems I had I was able to phone him up. For instance, one artist I had engaged reneged on the deal and wouldn't sign the contract and I was in danger of losing the theatres I had booked. Saunders gave me the right advice and it worked. It was all contained in his autobiography, **'The Mousetrap Man'** published in 1972. I must say that Peter Saunders treated me like a grandson, although he had had no children of his own and was an exceedingly kind man. I always called him my 'mentor' because he was always there if I needed him. There was also the lovely story that while I was desperate on one of my tours for finance, he bumped into me and said, 'How's it going?' He had heard about the play I was presenting and I had written to him to say, 'I'm very sorry but I could do with some backing.' He sent a cheque back straightaway. I thought *how nice*. He lost all of it because the tour was a disaster. He admitted that he could afford these tax losses because of the profits from the **'Mousetrap'** and he used to invest in a lot of shows.

He told me he owned eighty percent of the Mousetrap and a friend of mine who knew him said his sister had a small investment and was getting more per month than her state pension as a result of this. He said it had enabled him to have a trouble-free life because he had also bought theatres and he put on shows in which he lost money. Not everyone will know it but when John Gale got into problems with **'No Sex Please, We're British'**, Peter Saunders bought it off him. He had the longest running thriller and the longest running comedy in London and was a very astute man.

The Appropriate Theatre Investment Strategy?

He advised me to buy the rights of a play and I approached John Bedding at Samuel French, who got me my first, **'Murder by the Book'** and in addition to this found me a repertory theatre, the **Haymarket at Basingstoke** run by an Ian Mullins. (5) He agreed to put the play on to a professional standard if I could provide two names and they would let me take it out on tour to around X theatres, in return for a percentage of the tour profits, which was all very sensible. I still had of course, to fund putting the play together and pay my costs on the tour. The name of the game at the time was to use ex-actors from television in pretty safe dramas. The theatres would in those days give guarantees and everyone was happy. However, I did not get many of these guarantees although I got very good percentage deals such as eighty percent of the box office at the Birmingham Alexander Theatre for taking the risk with them, but I still had to find these named artists which were where the problem started. Saunders said that 'Even if you are well known like me if a film comes along you've had it, because an artist will go for the film'. Well eventually I got Ray Lonen who had been in **'Harry's Game,'** to play the male lead and of course he had been at the **Theatre Royal Stratford East** in **'A Christmas Carol'** when I was there, which was pure co-incidence. Then from the Tennant days, Elizabeth Seal who had been the original 'Irma La Douce' for which she had won a Tony Award in 1961. I met her agent who said, 'Well, she is looking for work and could be your leading lady.' I met her and she was absolutely wonderful. She was very valiant and she looked at the costs of going on tour to make sure that her costumes were not going to need washing every five minutes. I could not have wished for a better first lady. We opened at The Haymarket Theatre Basingstoke and it went on tour and there was also the financing of it which is why I wanted the agreement from Peter Saunders. We agreed to split £24,000 into £500 units and I sold over half to friends and the rest I put up myself with Marion Park who was a partner in this venture and the balance was on overdraft. These friends who took on £500 each were people such as Norman Sharp, fellow retailers and old school friends. Also, Roger Simpson, our very astute Wheatley-Ward family financial investment guru, who assisted me with one of his clients. They all had confidence in me because we actually owned the rights including the West End 'Murder by the Book', which was originally known as 'In at the Death,' when Ray Cooney started out as a Producer at the Phoenix Theatre, Shipman having taken over. I had worked on it with Nigel Hawthorne in the cast and it was a comedy murder which was very well received when it went out so much so that through Peter Saunders, J Herbert Jay who owned the Ambassadors Theatre came out to see it.

At one point it looked as if it could have headed for London but the young producer who was with Herbert Jay had a musical which he thought might be a better bet so it did not get anywhere near there. To be honest I would have had a job to find the £50,000 but it was nice to know that I was on the right track and it actually got my name about in the provincial theatre, that there was a producer out there who came out with decent sets and good acting. Thanks to Ian Mullins and his directorship, it was well put together and it gelled. Out of this tour I gained more contacts including John Goodrum, whose wife was on the stage management at the Haymarket Basingstoke. My company manager was John Short, who was a member of the Jimmy Logan theatre family. Also, I began a life-long friendship with Keith Salberg, who became another mentor. Finally, Billy Differ who helped me book the King's Theatre Glasgow, which financially saved the tour. He rose to become Operations Director for Cameron Mackintosh's west end theatres. I also joined the **'The Theatrical Managers' Association (TMA)**, meeting other producers, some of whom I felt most uncomfortable with. During the run of this tour I was in the shop in Windsor and who walked in to buy a blazer but Mr Jolyon Jackley the young general manager of the **Theatre Royal Windsor**, (7) with whom we could not avoid talking about theatre. We hit it off from the start and became pals.

Theatre Royal Windsor (Theatres Trust)

He wanted out from the Theatre Royal because he was getting bored with dealing with a set of trustees. So he assisted me with contacts and we looked at other projects, including buying theatres. I did another tour of a play called **'A Fish out of Water'** and also invested in other productions, but overall, I am the first to admit that although I was losing money I was gaining experience. I was introduced to an American playwright Lewis Dickson, who wanted help to stage his plays. He had been a past vice-president of American Express. I did approach The Arts Council about funding touring drama, which was not taken up through my alleged lack of suitable experience in this field! Putting a commercial tour together was not as easy as it sounds for casting the play also involves booking the theatres. On phoning these theatres you eventually get through to the manager as another 'Joe Soap' producer, of which there were quite a few at that time and they had lots of people to choose from. It occurred to me and I said this to Jolyon, that if we had our own theatre it would be better for me to start shows off in it. Then go about saying far and wide, 'We are the theatre would you like our show?' We actually looked at the West End to start with because Jolyon had lots of contacts there and we were after the **Whitehall**. We also looked at the elegant Edwardian Playhouse of Italian renaissance style, the **Southsea Kings Theatre**. (8) There is a lovely Reginald Cooper story told to me by Henry Magee about when he was at the Southsea King's Theatre for a press conference. There is this young very well dressed and well-built female reporter at one corner of the Circle Bar and **Reginald Cooper** was at the other end of the bar. He went over and started to chat her up and he was in his seventies. Now you may not think that is amusing but when I tell you that he was on his Zimmer frame and that he had every intention of getting this girl to bed, you can see the funny side of it.

He still had that spark in his old mind and he was just an old rogue like so many of them! When we toured **'Murder by the Book'**, to Southsea, my partner Marion Park, asked for our settlement cheque on the last night which was not forthcoming. Marion said the tabs were not going up on the second act until it was produced and the cheque instantaneously appeared. Reginald Cooper made his money by inventing a device that halved the diesel consumption in naval vessels and I remember my grandfather at RAE Farnborough, telling me he had heard of this gentleman as it annoyed the petrol companies for obvious reasons. We met the old commander Reginald Cooper, who was one of the most notorious men in the business for cheque bouncing and other problems but who was 'a dear old soul'. He also owned the **Theatre Royal Portsmouth**, (9) whose first post-war manager was a Leslie Pace whom I met when he was manager of the ABC Windsor. The Theatre Royal Portsmouth did not have the use of its stage as something had happened and it burnt down as children had been allowed by Reggie Cooper to play with fireworks on it. What was quite spooky is the safety curtain descended of its own accord, saving this theatre. **(See Chapter 6 – Some Phantoms of the Theatre)**

Theatre Royal Portsmouth (Theatre Trust Archives)

Auditorium of the New Theatre Royal Portsmouth (Theatres Trust

When I was involved with the trust some years ago to save it again, I asked about the clause that Reggie Cooper had put in when he owned the Theatre Royal Portsmouth. On selling it this clause stated that it could not be used for live theatre any more because he wanted to encourage more business for the King's Theatre Southsea, which he also owned. The bureaucrats at the council were amazed that I knew about that secret clause. When the Southsea Kings went bust I helped re-start it which again enabled it to attain the success it has today, now known as **'King's Theatre Portsmouth.'**

King's Portsmouth (From Theatres Trust Archives)

By now I had my own businesses and felt secure but I didn't fancy the West End again so with Jolyon I started to look in the Estates Gazette for a theatre to buy somewhere else. One day this old theatre that I had known since my youth the **Theatre Royal Margate**, was up for auction. The most famous actress manager here was **Sarah Thorne**. I went rushing to Jolyon and I said 'You'll never believe it, the theatre I knew as a kid is on the market in Margate?' He replied, 'I know Margate from my youth!' Consequently, the very next thing was that we were going down to view it. A further study of both the Theatre Royal and Margate as a seaside town would enable a greater understanding of some of the factors which have contributed to its success and failure since first opening in 1787. Some of these details are to be found in the next chapter of this book.

References

1. **The New Empire Theatre Alexandra Street Southend-on-Sea** opened in 1896 on the site of the old public hall with plush seats and private boxes. It has existed as three different buildings and according to the 'Spooky Evenings' website, is one of the scariest places. The theatre holds a catalogue of unexplained but tragic events of sound and light images. More recently it has been a commercial success for ghost hunters. The fate of this theatre is now in question after it was almost destroyed by a fire in 2007 deliberately started, destroying the roof and Victorian first floor pavilion.

2. According to wikipedia, The **Saville Theatre** at 135 Shaftesbury_Avenue"Shaftesbury Avenue in the "London Borough of Camden was designed by the architect Thomas_Bennett_(architect)"Sir Thomas Bennett and opened on 8 October 1931, with a play with music by H.F._Maltby"H.F. Maltby, *For The Love Of Mike*. In the 1960s it became a music venue and in 1970, the two cinemas **ABC1 Shaftesbury Avenue** and **ABC2 Shaftesbury Avenue**, which in 2001 were converted to the four-screen cinema **Odeon Covent Garden.** The original theatre had 1,426 seats on three levels and a stage that was 31.5 feet (9.6 m) wide, with a depth of 30.5 feet (9.3 m). The interior was opulent with an extremely comfortable bar. The exterior of the theatre depicts a frieze by British sculptor

3. **There's a Girl in My Soup** – was a comedy written by Terrance Frisby which won the Writers' of Great Britain award and ran from 1966 to 1972 at the Globe Theatre (now the **Gielgud**) London starring Donald Sinden, Barbara Ferris and Jon Pertwee, breaking all records as the world's longest running comedy. The film in 1970 starred Peter Sellars, Tony Britten, Goldie Hawn and Diana Dors.

4. **'Queue Sera Sera' – Whatever will be will be** introduced by the American actress Doris Day in the 1956 film **'The Man Who Knew Too Much'**.

5. **Sir Peter Saunders** was the original producer of Agatha Christie's 'Mousetrap', which opened at the Theatre Royal Nottingham in 1952, based on her short story 'Three Blind Mice'. He had remarked to Agatha Christie that it would only play for about fourteen months and she replied that it would probably be less than that. It opened in London's Ambassadors Theatre in London on 25th November 1952 and transferred

next door to St Martin's Theatre in 1974, where it has continued to play ever since. He followed his older brother, Charles Saunders who was a film director, into show-business as firstly a cameraman and then a director. He had work as a newspaper reporter and as press agent to Harry Roy. He served in the Second World War as an Army Captain in the Intelligence Corps, moving into theatre production as hostilities ceased. He purchased the **Vaudeville Theatre** in 1969 and took out a long lease on London's **St Martins Theatre**. He also had owned the **Duchess Theatre** and the **Duke of Yorks.**

6. The Haymarket Theatre Basingstoke
The Haymarket Theatre opened in 1951 and was refurbished and re-opened in October 1993. Originating as a Corn Exchange in 1865 and much later a roller rink and a theatre. In 1913 it became a grand cinema having a Will Hammer lease until 1950. The building was burnt down in 1925 and due to public demand, it was rebuilt.

7. The Theatre Royal Windsor
This is the third of three theatres which have existed in Windsor (apart from a theatre on Peascod Street a mile out of town on a 21-year lease from 1787). The first was built in 1793 on the High Street and opened on the 'glorious twelfth' of August with Mrs Brainchild's Comedy 'Everyone has His Fault'. It was followed by the farce 'Rosina' in the presence of King George III and members of the royal family who were residing at Windsor castle. The cast were invited afterwards to a royal supper at the castle. The theatre after falling into dilapidation was renovated in 1869 although it was only open for the summer season. In 1805 it was sold and was converted into a chapel which outraged many local residents who set up a campaign to fund the building as a new theatre project.

This second theatre was opened on Thames Street on 22nd August 1815 with a production of 'School for Scandal' having been host to a preview for Queen Charlotte and several members of the royal family. A bizarre and fatal incident involving a lady of 63 falling off the gallery and into the pit breaking her back took place in 1845. By 1869 the theatre was in a dilapidated state having been closed for some time and bought by a Mr J. Freemantle who was a member of a local amateur group called 'The Windsor Strollers', who engaged an architect Somers Clark to restore it. This involved demolishing the old pit and gallery entrance and replacing it with a new one. Although a small theatre the design was a colourful red and black in Pompeian style. The theatre was further renovated in 1900 and renamed the 'Theatre Royal and Opera House,' with plush seating in the dress circle and tip-up seats in the upper circle. Sadly, this theatre was completely destroyed by fire eight years later in 1908. However, by 1910 Sir William Shirley and a Captain Reginald Shipley had opened a new theatre on this site on 13th December 1910, which still stands to this day.

8. Kings Theatre Southsea

This is an elegant Edwardian playhouse owned by Portsmouth Theatre Company of which Frank Matcham was the architect opened in 1907 with 'Charles 1' and two of Henry Irving's works. In 1964 it was bought by a Commander and Mrs Reggie Cooper and sold to Hampshire Council 1n 1990. A restoration company was set up to keep it open and it came under the ownership of Portsmouth City Council and leased to the Kings Theatre Trust. The tower of this 1,600 seat theatre was restored in 2009.

9. The New Theatre Royal Portsmouth

Now the re-born 'New Theatre Royal' was originally constructed in 1854 as Landport Hall. Henry Rutley a travelling circus proprietor bought the 'Swan Tavern' now the 'White Swan', which adjoined it and gained a licence to convert the hall into a theatre which opened in September 1856. In 1884 it was substantially rebuilt and redesigned by the architect Charles Phipps who designed the circular balcony with levels similar to the Theatre Royal Bath. In 1900 Frank Matcham (previously mentioned as the designer of Hackney Empire and other London theatres) extended the Dress Circle and also added pairs of boxes at dress and balcony levels. The New Theatre Royal brochure mentions this as one of three remaining examples in Europe (Tivoli in Aberdeen and the Theatre Royal Nottingham) which reflect the creativity of both Charles Phipps and Frank Matcham. It has been designated a Grade II listed building by English Heritage. The stage was partly destroyed by fire in 1972 but mysteriously, the safety curtain lowered and saved the theatre. Later some vandalism occurred to the plaster work and fixtures and it has been operating for over forty years with a temporary stage, as well as severely limited backstage facilities. It has had many periods in dark and at one time was used as a wrestling hall. This reborn theatre is the merger of nineteenth century with a twenty-first century stage house. Now with improved backstage facilities contemporary bar and seating for 700 including wheelchair spaces at all levels. This represents a joint venture between the **New Theatre Royal Management** and the **University of Portsmouth** with a synergy of ambitions for a working professional theatre aligned with a faculty of performing arts. **This theatre is also featured by Raymond Lamont Brown in 'Phantoms of the Theatre'- Satellite Books 1977 and appeared in the Theatre Trusts Magazine**

10. The Bangor Theatre

Was originally the Tabernacle Chapel was built in 1850 and closed in 1911. It was purchased by Mr. James Hare who converted it into a theatre by adding a stage 30 feet in width by 40 feet in depth, including a fly tower and a small foyer. The existing chapel balcony was converted allowing seating for 846 people. It opened in 1912 as the New County Theatre showing films with two changes of programme per week at prices from 6d Talking pictures a Western Electric Sound system was installed and seat prices rose to 1/6d. (From Wikipeadia)

Chapter 4 – A Background History of the Theatre Royal Margate

The background history of both the **Theatre Royal** and Margate as a seaside town would enable a greater understanding of some of the factors which have contributed to its success and failure since first opening in 1787. A book entitled **'Margate and its Theatres' by Malcolm Morley** published in 1966, recalls the Theatre Royal Margate having had a precarious history and being 'dark', for several lengthy periods. The biographer acknowledges with much appreciation Ian Carter-Chapman, who has researched the history of the Theatre Royal for many years on which he now lectures. He has painstakingly collated much detail in a number of scrapbooks of some previous productions, especially during the tenure of the subject of this book, Michael Wheatley-Ward, which will also be referred to in Chapter 5. He has greatly assisted in verifying the accuracy of the information included in both these chapters.

Acknowledging that seaside locations are prone to the dictates of weather and seasonality affecting their visitor numbers this also affects the demand for entertainment. **Malcolm Morley** relates that in the late 1700s the wealthy visited resorts for the health-giving properties of sea bathing and in land spa towns such as Tunbridge Wells and Bath. During their stay they also sought the use of libraries, assembly rooms for functions and subscription ballrooms. In Margate the first Assembly Room was on the parade at the **'Black Horse Inn,'** which opened in 1754 and was later taken over by a John Mitchener, who in 1761, added a hotel to this site. By 1769, he was experiencing competition from a new assembly room and hotel at 'New Square,' later known as **'Cecil Square'**. This **'Smiths Hotel'** became **'Fox Hotel'**, **'Smiths Tavern'**, **'Benson Hotel'** and after 1794, the **'Royal Hotel'**. The significance of this historical information is that this site would much later house the **'New Grand Theatre,'** later **'The Hippodrome'**, that for a time would be regarded as a competitor to the **'Theatre Royal'**, which later detail in this chapter will verify.

The landlord of **'The Fountain Inn'** King's Street was a Francis Cobb, also the head of Cobbs Brewery and regarded as an intellectual businessman. At the reenthe Fountain Inn was a stable containing a performing space, rented for £20 per year by a retired sea captain, Charles Mate. In the street outside performers would encourage the public to become an audience by donning their comic robes, powdered heads and painting their faces. They had to compete for their audience's attention with animal noises such as horses and barking dogs in the stable. To meet these challenges Charles Mate decided to invest £200 and open a purpose-built theatre on this site. A Sarah Baker from a theatrical family company based in Dover, considered to be the first female theatre manager; broached Mr Cobb in 1785 with the idea of opening a theatre in Margate and he flatly refused to support it. In retaliation she had erected a temporary wooden theatre costing £500, in just over a month for that summer season.

Within three months of opening his season Charles Mate found this competition to be too strong since he was losing money so he lost interest and returned to his theatre in Dover. Mr. Cobb arranged a petition which was signed by 900 local towns' people to parliament, requesting a **Royal Charter. 'The Margate Playhouse Bill'** was introduced and a Royal Charter awarded which gave the licensee the power to send Mrs. Baker back to Dover and prevented other companies setting up arbitrarily in Margate thereafter. Charles Mate was determined to try again having previously formed a partnership with Thomas Robson, a singer from Covent Garden London. Opening his former Margate Theatre, he named the **'Theatre Royal,'** which was to be closed only a year later due to the preparations underway for a permanent new Theatre Royal at a new site, on the east side of Hawley Street at the junction of Princes Street, now known as **'Addington Street'**. Malcolm Morely further relates that just nine months after laying the foundation stone in September 1786 and after construction costs of £4,000, a ceremonial opening took place on June 27th 1787. In the late reign of George III actors, had gained some respectability and could even be regarded as **'His Majesty's Servants;'** enabling them to wear royal livery at special occasions, in major contrast to previous times when they were regarded as 'rogues' and 'vagabonds'. The Theatre Royal could and did display the royal coat of arms on its portico. The very first production **'She Stoops to Conquer'**, a literary favourite by **Oliver Goldsmith,** had originally opened in London's **Covent Garden Theatre** on March 15th 1773. London productions would now tour the provincial circuit of which Margate was a part, providing all public performances had been approved beforehand by the local magistrates. At the Theatre Royal the first management team were Messrs Robinson as manager, Booth the finances as well as taking small acting parts, together with a determined Charles Mate, who painted scenery and was also 'stage man. Outbreak of fire in theatres at this time was a high risk. Miraculously it occurred only once and on a small scale at the Theatre Royal Margate behind some scenery, on August 15th 1789 and was rapidly extinguished. Margate had been one of the first coastal resorts identified for sea bathing; as advocated by a Dr Richard Russell, to improve all ailments even for invalids as well as holiday makers. Some were even brave enough to drink sea water as well as bathe in it. A Sea Bathing Hospital was founded in 1791, whereas thirty years previously only bathing rooms had existed on the beach. Attractions such as these meant that by the end of the eighteenth century the population of the town exceeded 5,000 in the summer, with visitors raising the demand for entertainment of quality. The key to success would be to choose proven performing theatre companies and old favourite productions with talented young actors who would be engaged each summer. Most plays had been originally staged at either London's Drury Lane or Covent Garden Theatres. A typical main play would be of five acts as a sentimental rendering of the failure of true love and in the last act all difficulties would be resolved. Popular authors at this time were Thomas Morton, Richard Cumberland and Charles Dibdin and familiar titles were **'The Quaker'**, **'Love in a Village'**, **'Rosina'** and plays by Shakespeare. There were also comedies by Sheridan and Goldsmith and **'The Beggars' Opera',** originating in 1728 by John Gay, to the music of George Frederick Handel.

Local talent could also gain some recognition since a Margate librarian whose name was Garner, was an actor who played Shylock in **'The Merchant of Venice'** and as a result, he acquired the name round the town from thereafter as 'Old Shylock'.

London players found Margate a profitable place to perform in during summer as the London Theatres were closed and only a perfunctory rehearsal was required with the star actor before the run at the seaside began. Prior to the Napoleonic War, army and naval personnel had a battalion in Birchington and officers frequented the boxes and the pit at the Theatre Royal and soldiers in the gallery. Margate became prosperous by attracting visitors due to its easy access to the continent. There were popular masquerade balls at the **'Assembly Rooms'**, near the seafront, (these being the first Assembly Rooms). However, the Theatre Royal was closed during the winter months and at the onset of the Napoleonic Wars in 1792 as attendance started to decline, reportedly due to competition from games involving dice! This encouraged the Theatre Royal to join the Dover Theatre circuit from which it was operated but retaining some autonomy to maintain its own independence. In 1803 the theatre was conscripted and occupied as an auxiliary barracks but the following summer it was returned to the proprietor to be re-opened again as a theatre. From the chronology of management can be seen that all ran relatively smoothly until the end of the Saville Faucit period 1820 to 1840. They divorced although they had had a family of six children and for about a year the theatre was used as a chapel, with pews and a pulpit, replacing the auditorium seats.

However, from July 1842 a re-dressed re-seated theatre was again re-opened by a J D. Robson owner of the Royal Hotel. Thomas Noon Talfourd, a friend of Charles Dickens, wrote a tragedy entitled, **'The Athenian Captive'** and presented it at the Theatre Royal. Dickens who was spending the summer at what he called, his 'waterhole' in Broadstairs and came to see this tragedy, stating that he had even been prepared to walk the eight miles in order to see it! Somewhat surprisingly he made fun of it (which was apparently his habit with country theatricals). It was ironic that the restrictions under the Charter of 1786 were to be over-ruled in 1843, which set all theatres on an equal footing being no longer dependent upon a Royal Patent. Instead, licences were renewable by local authorities and would be granted on a yearly basis. However, the Theatre Royal was to remain dark for some two years until in 1845 when Joseph Combs (1) opened it enthusiastically with a much repeated **'Pizarro'** and a melodrama by Edward Fiz entitled **'Jonathan Bradford'**.

Perhaps unsurprisingly the demand for tickets was slim and at a later production of **'Othello'**, two well-known actors did not turn up for the performance. Consequently, **'The Merry Wives of Windsor'** was proposed to the assembled audience as a substitute, which they verbally rejected, which prompted one of the company to come on stage to explain to the audience that **Joseph Combes**, the theatre manager, had left with all the takings!

The theatre again re-opened on Boxing Day in 1842, firstly with a melodrama **'Blanche Heriot'** by Albert Smith, which was a sensation and was followed by the very first pantomime, **'Ride a Cock Horse to Banbury Cross'**. At this time opening at Christmas would have been a contravention of the official regulations and dates for action under the 'Charter of 1786'. Remarkably however this Charter did not apply to amateurs, who seem to have been granted magistrate's licences automatically. Robson, the then manager, was ordered to close the theatre yet again, so he took his company to Canterbury where these restrictions did not apply.

Malcolm Morely's research acknowledges that the Assembly Rooms in Cecil Square nearby had experienced declining business in this same period. Also, that although theatres were now able to open all the year round it was still only during the summer that there were sufficient numbers of theatre-goers in Margate to justify any entertainment on offer. Easier travelling especially by rail would lead to extensive touring by theatrical companies and by 1855 it would be Richard Thorne, later followed by one of his daughters Sarah Thorne, who would set up a residential company in Margate which would determine the passage of drama for more than fifty years. Richard Thorne had learnt the art of entertaining the masses if not the classes from his own father G. H. Thorne, from an early age which included fitting up both portable and permanent stages. He had even rented some northern theatres at Bolton, Blackburn and Preston and had managed the **Pavilion Theatre** in Whitechapel London for several years. (1) He had a 'colourful' personality, was fond of gambling and often wore dandified dress.

THE NEW ROYAL PAVILION THEATRE, WHITECHAPEL-ROAD.

He married a Sarah Rogers of Rotherhithe and their daughter, another Sarah, was a child actress at the Pavilion. He became the lessee of the Theatre Royal Margate at the age of forty-two and had it more thoroughly decorated than ever before and installed three glass chandeliers in the auditorium and engaged a resident company for a season of between ten and twelve weeks. By this time amateur theatricals commencing in Canterbury had also been growing rapidly throughout Kent. A re-opening of a refurbished Theatre Royal took place on July 28th 1855 and on August 6th, when Sarah Thorne at less than twenty made her début at Margate as Pauline in Lord Lytton's verse drama, **'The Lady of Lyons.'** In the 1859 season Richard's sons Richard Jr., 19 and Tom, 17, had also become a major part of the company. Sarah presented a lecture on the 'Amusement and Claim of the Drama' which was to occupy one and a half hours as this was the outcome of her studies.

In 1856 Charles Morton completed a new Assembly Rooms and the Tivoli Gardens (research shows this to be a different Charles Morton to the founder of the Canterbury and Oxford Music Halls in London). Possibly due to this competition during the first season, the box office was disappointing but his daughter **Sarah Thorne**, persuaded him to try for just one further season to see if there would be an improvement. There was and the Theatre Royal from thereon gained its place as a valuable asset to Margate. By 1857 Richard Thorne had several of his ten children on the Margate stage performing in tried favourites such as **'The Green Bushes'** and **'The Lost Ship'**, although for the remainder of the year the theatre was largely out of action, apart from occasional concert evenings, meetings or amateur performances. In Canterbury a company known as **'The Old Stagers'** was very popular and continued on to become one of the longest-lived amateur companies. Margate was to see a number of stars during that season from the London stages and those playing supporting roles assigned to them in advance, were expected to know the text for a run-through with the star. They were also expected to find their own way round the stage, being permitted to move anywhere provided that they did not interfere with the actions of that star. The Theatre Royal gradually became popular in the summer with touring companies and sometimes for periods in winter and was constantly in use with a growing number of amateur companies, the most predominant being 'The Margate Dramatic Club.' There were many notable productions during Richard Thorne's tenure later assisted by his daughter Sarah. A melodrama in 1861 with a water cave involving a large water tank on stage. Drama which was highly commended with names such as Charles Harcourt, Ersser Jones, C. H. Stephenson, Kate Rivers, Patty Oliver, John Colman, James Bennett and Celeste. At this time burlesque was gaining popularity in London and arrived in Margate in 1862 and involving extreme liberties being taken with established works and male and female roles often reversed. An outrageous burlesque might follow a solemn classical work. Sarah Thorne had been praised for not being 'too stagey' in her portrayal of Pauline in **'The Lady of Lyons.'** Significantly the Thorne family were to become prominent on the Theatre Royal stage, with Sarah especially invited to perform in other towns as well. She proved to be a versatile but believable performer, playing Lady Gay Spanker in the comedy **'London Assurance'** and sometimes boy parts in burlesque.

In the meantime, a young George Thorne also took parts before he was later to become associated with the **D'Oyly Carte Opera Company**. However, by 1866 Richard Thorne was seeking to relinquish some responsibilities and make for a phased retirement. He even sub-leased the theatre to a Florence Webster which was not a success and which ended her association with the Theatre Royal. Richard Thorne, although dubious about continuing the lease, was to transfer it to his ambitious daughter Sarah, who from 1867 to 1873 became the manager.

The Importance of the Railways

South Eastern Railway had a direct line from Fenchurch Street to Margate and the journey took two hours with rivalry existing between steam transport and other railway companies. The Chatham and Dover Railway constructed a line that was to have a terminus near Margate beach. However, the Margate authorities refused to sanction it because this line crossed the South Eastern Railway. The outcome was that this unused station was converted by a catering company Spiers and Pond, into a place of entertainment and dance hall, under the name of **'Hall by the Sea'**. (2) This building was used for variety of concerts as was the Assembly Rooms and artists of note were engaged. Entertainment was also on offer at Dryson's in the High Street which was often described as the first music hall proper in Margate. However, the Assembly Rooms and the Hall by the Sea were regarded as the main competitors of the Theatre Royal when Sarah Thorne took over in 1867. Although she performed in other parts of the country her heart and home were in Margate. The theatre underwent a further transformation with the Boxes and the Dress Circle for the first time being provided with cushioned seats giving an emphasis on greater comfort. Even the much-acclaimed gas chandeliers were discarded as well as the old front curtain and instead there was throughout a prevalence of new decoration and cleanliness. The popularity of the Theatre Royal was to continue during the first six years of Sarah Thorne's management which at the start she had described it as 'a ship leaving the harbour spreading her sails in the breeze'. Her own notable performances were Meg in **'Meg's Diversion'** by H. T. Craven and **'The Child of the Regiment'**, using the music of Donizetti's opera **'La Fille du Regiment'**. She also played the blind Iolanthe in **'King Rene's Daughter,'** which was a poetic rendering of Danish origin. The theatre was full from floor to roof with an audience who would applaud the débutante manageress. The 1868 season had contemporary players such as Toole, Charles Mathews, John Clarke, Teresa Furtado and the French actress Mlle Beatrice who played in English the classic Marie Stuart of Schiller. There was also a predominance of Shakespearian plays. In Margate entertainment was flourishing everywhere starting with minstrels on the sands, the one-hundred-year-old Assembly Rooms at Cecil Square, now came under the direction of Edwin Villiers from south London, who emphasised that on offer here was a much higher class of entertainment than the Halls by the Sea! Also, some notorieties such as J. L. Toole and Henry Irving (3) who were rarely apart and being on an extensive tour came to Margate for a 'holiday'.

In the 1871 season a new leading man Walter Roberts was outstanding as Micawber in **'David Copperfield'** and **Quilp** in **'The Old Curiosity Shop'**.

Malcolm Morely states that the yearly rental for the Theatre Royal was £135 and 4 shillings, including the rental for the adjacent house in which Sarah was living and including a shop. Unbeknown to her the property had been put up for auction and sold to the highest bidder, caterer, Robert Fort, who was not a theatre man, although he had an actress wife. In consequence the Theatre Royal Margate underwent a run of managements between 1874 and 1878 although the attraction of Margate as a holiday destination continued despite the changes taking place on the entertainment scene. The Hall by the Sea which had never been profitable was purchased by a Lord George Sanger a showman and owner of an English founded circus. Circus animals could be lodged in the grounds and be tended to when they fell sick. The main building could be rented out for concerts and exhibitions and space was also available as a show place for relics and curiosities. The new proprietor of the Theatre Royal, Robert Fort, spent about £10,000 on alterations which were carried out by J. T. Robinson, who was designer of the 1871 **'Old Vic'** auditorium. Kebler's Margate and Ramsgate Gazette described the refurbished Theatre Royal as one of the prettiest theatres ever seen! In Robert Fort's view the front entrance was unsightly so he had it bricked up and replaced by what is still in use to this day and considered as a 'circular corner of indiscriminate architecture' in Addington Street. Inside there were separate ways to the boxes, the dress circle and the pit. The interior design was a pleasant white and gold and there was a refreshment room at the back of the circle, the front being carpeted with a promenade considered to be the epitome of luxury.

Although Fort had intended to run the theatre himself, he considered it wiser to ask Sarah Thorne to be the director and including responsibility for the management of productions. This she readily accepted this although it reduced her previous authority. After another 'grand opening', on July 10th 1874 and afterwards a ceremonial rendering of the national anthem followed by the comedy **'Coals of Fire,'** by Craven. Then a ballet divertimento and a regulation farce. **(8)** As Sarah feared, Mrs Fort (who was formerly Harriet Wilson), had a large say in the selection of pieces especially those that would display her vocal abilities. Sarah having previously been the captain of the ship now found herself taking orders as the petty officer and even being directed on how she should direct. Mrs Fort sang the title role in **'Joan of Arc'** by Offenbach which was not greatly appreciated, or the extravaganza **'Lallah Rookh'**. Consequently, the season was brought to an early close in September and Sarah arranged to take the theatre back from Fort in the short term and tour some provincial cities. She returned back that Christmas to produce a pantomime which was also toured for three nights each to Maidstone, Ramsgate and Sandwich and other places seeking Christmas entertainment. Instructing amateurs in theatre was to set the seed for her later famous **'School of Acting'**. Another major policy change in 1875 was that the theatre would not be run principally for the summer season only but throughout the year, as now touring companies had spread everywhere and were invited to apply for any available dates.

The terms were a direct rental or a percentage of takings. Fort now leased the theatre to an H. E. Davis, a local man, who was to take sole responsibility for the next three months. He engaged Virginia Blackwood and Murray Wood her husband who had been touring the country for several years, she having performed both Little Nell and the Marchioness in the **'Old Curiosity Shop.'** Somewhat unexpectedly Davis pulled out of the Theatre Royal and transferred his attention to another venue the **Oriental Music Hall**, of which he became the proprietor, re-naming it **'The Prince of Wales Concert Rooms'**. An Edward Price on becoming the lessee on June 19th re-named the Royal the **'New Theatre and Opera House'**. Although Edward Price was an actor in secondary roles in London, he obtained lead roles in the provinces. However, at the end of this season, the Theatre Royal was advertised as 'To Be Let' at a rental of £800 per annum and taken up by a Frank Musgrave in 1876. During that summer there were a succession of stars such as Harry Simms as Squeers in **'Nicholas Nickelby'**, Ada Cavendish as Mercy Merrick in the **'New Magdalen'** by Wilkie Collins and many more. Sarah Thorne and her sister Emily (Mrs McKnight) were in **'She Stoops to Conquer.'** After this Sarah was to embark on the travelling pantomime and as Mrs McKnight, she lived at 5 Hawley Square Margate. The actress Ellen Ternan considered to be associated with Charles Dickens since the production of Wilkie Collin's play **'The Frozen Deep'** in Manchester, also came to live in Margate and had an unbroken friendship with Charles Dickens which continued until his death in 1870. In 1876 she married a George Robinson who established himself as headmaat the Margate High School in Hawley Street which was to be their home for ten years. Ellen taught elocution to the pupils and gave readings from Dickens works, as well as directing performances of Shakespeare.

A Second Term Lease for Sarah Thorne

Malcolm Morely mentions that Robert Fort's tenure was unsuccessful and he was glad to lease the theatre to Sarah Thorne, who was to be given a free hand to run it and be a reliable tenant. From her childhood days at the Pavilion in London's East End, she had developed her yearning for the theatre and whilst still young, had been regarded as a leading actress in provincial playhouses.

Sarah Thorne 1836-1899

However, she had a desire to develop latent talent in others and particularly the young. She had rented a theatre in Worcester for nearly twenty years before returning to make Margate her home. She had met a Scotsman Thomas McKnight who although a divorcee, she married and they had two children: Edmund in 1859 and Elizabeth, known as 'Bessie', in 1861. Edmund would eventually be a business manager and Bessie an actress. Although the marriage of Sarah and Thomas had been a love match at the start, serious differences would develop.

Sarah found it difficult to be the dutiful wife of a literary man, a politician and an editor of a journal entitled **'The Northern Whig'**. Inevitably they agreed to separate, he remaining in Belfast and she gravitating to Margate, to be followed later by her children. Again taking over the Theatre Royal her aim was to make it viable, both in summer and winter, because when not providing productions herself, there were by now more than one hundred national touring companies to call upon. Provincial players were encouraged to copy the London actors in their roles and these touring companies often had their own scenery to replicate a London production.

The railways even provided discounted fares together with trucks for the transportation of scenery for performances that were generally for three nights. Some actors and actresses even had their own companies and offered a repertory of plays to be performed on different nights with the novices under their tutelage. In her returning season Sarah Thorne played Julia in **'The Hunchback'** with her own company. The regular season commenced from July 21st to October 4th and the actors engaged were Frank Rodney, J. S. Blythe, F. W. Sidney, Nina Cressy, Ellen Leigh, Mrs C. Jones and Edward Compton (who was the father of Compton Mackenzie and Fay Compton). First on the bill was the Buckstone's comedy **'Leap Year'** and Bouciaults's **'The Flying Scud.'** The regular season would only be interrupted when the highly popular, D'Oyly Carte Company arrived with **'H.M.S. Pinafore,'** the resident members of that company being located in Dover. There were many stars of the London stage that were happy to perform in Margate and on the list in 1879 were Ada Swanborough, H. M. Vernon, Lionel Brough, Kyrle Bellew and the comedian Toole. At Easter in 1880 W. H.

Hallet brought his theatre company touring with **'Alive or Dead'** and Robert Hall's adaptation of the unfinished novel **'The Mystery of Edwin Drood'** by Charles Dickens. Hallet's talented son Henry was an accomplished actor who played leading roles both in London and the provinces. Sarah Thorne in this year had also been involved in the management of Astley's Amphitheatre and had also been acting before she returned back to Margate for the season with a new drama by George W. Browne entitled, **'A King of Shreds and Patches'**.

Sale of Liquor at the Theatre Royal

It is interesting to note that the licence to sell liquor was still under the jurisdiction of the Lord Chamberlain and that sales might only be suspended for one hour during the day and the theatre was open to all and sundry. Often drinking would take place in the small hours of which Sarah disapproved, especially by actors, whilst acknowledging it as a source of revenue for the theatre. However, when she received an offer from a local victualler to take over the sale of alcohol she transferred the official sanction to him, deeming her no longer responsible.

An innovative surprise to the audience in 1881 was a new act drop, with all manner of advertisements including forthcoming productions instead of just a painting. This was obviously a means of advertising the season and possibly gaining advertising fees from traders as well. The strength of Sarah Thorne's long tenure was that few productions were new and untried but had been well tested and approved by previous theatre audiences. She accepted somewhat reluctantly, audiences' growing demand for weepy plays and even played in them, although she preferred the old costumed comedies by Sheridan, Goldsmith and Shakespeare. It was this formula which prevailed and kept the theatre viable. After Christmas came productions from good quality amateur groups, then there was a lull before Easter. Organisations on the road were booked until the start of the 'regular' or 'stock' season, which began in July for ten weeks. Then came the touring companies and during the Christmas holidays a travelling pantomime, whilst every year the D'Oyly Carte Opera

Company continued with the latest Gilbert and Sullivan work. Sarah Thorne was a capable business woman as well as a hard worker conversant with every aspect theatrical delivery and administration, as well as having good humour and tact. Her son Edmund or Edwin as he was sometimes known, helped in the box office and some of the routine business and after three years he was appointed General Manager, a position he maintained throughout his mother's lengthy tenancy. Sarah's company of players recruited each summer for the stock period also became a wandering tribe, who filled the odd weeks replacing a touring company who might at the last minute be unable to deliver. In 1882 the Royal Hotel and the Assembly Rooms built in 1769 were victims of a ferocious fire enhanced by a strong east wind also destroying other Georgian houses on the south side of Cecil Square. The Assembly Rooms had been available for meetings and very much for the use of local politics as was 'Forester's Concert Rooms'. Apart from a few walls of the Assembly Rooms left standing the site was to remain neglected in the centre of Margate for some years.

On 16th August 1883 the Theatre Royal performed Vanbrugh's costumed comedy **'The Provoked Husband'** with Henry Dundas (a young provincial actor) as Lord Townly, who played opposite Sarah Thorne as Lady Townly and her daughter Bessie, was also in the cast. This production was highly approved by critics in Margate. Bessie and Henry Dundas were eventually married and would continue the histrionic line since they had a daughter Elizabeth, who became the wife of Henry Oscar. Mr and Mrs Dundas were destined to run their own theatre company and tour the country when they were not involved at Margate. For six years the Theatre Royal prospered and other entertainment competitors such as Sanger's **'Hall by the Sea'** also did well with exhibitions, menagerie and waxworks, dances and concerts.

England's First School of Acting – Established 1885

Number Hawley Square was not big enough for a school of acting so Sarah Thorne went for 'The Towers' in the same square, wrongly assumed to have been occupied by Horatio Nelson and Lady Hamilton. The school was advertised, 'For ladies and gentlemen wishing to enter the acting profession!' The focus was on strong discipline at a fee of £20 for three months or £30 for six months. Those showing specific talent after graduating were enlisted in the Theatre Royal with a salary of thirty shillings per week. This training in Margate might enable them to gain a walk-on part in London's West End and of course they could always return during the summer season to be welcomed back to Margate, where Sarah Thorne would be proud to bill them as alumni at their 'own metropolitan theatre!' This school which was the first of its kind was successful from the start and many prominent players graduated from it. The pupils or 'pupes' as they described themselves, had daily classes for instruction in the rudiments of acting, voice production, gesture, mime, dialects, accents, make-up, together with the importance of pace and pauses in the delivery of dialogue. Crucially the focus was the development of one's own personality in order to progress in the acting profession. Students would attend an evening performance in the theatre, in order to learn from those who were on stage but also more importantly, listen to the remarks and reaction from the audience as a learning exercise. Sunday was a free day without rehearsals when Sarah in her best attire conducted the pupes to church and back again and any malingering was disallowed. After church parade there was a party at the Towers where the students met the performers at the theatre in an enlivened but sedate manner. Sometimes Sarah was assisted in her teaching by her sister Emily, who had been acting in America for some years. She had married a Frances Parker Gilmore and their son Frank was to make his début at the Theatre Royal Margate that same year in 1885, in one of the many adaptations of Hugh Conway's popular novel, **'Called Back'**. Later another protégé of Sarah, Charles Rock, appeared in an adaptation of Florence Warden's popular novel, **'The House on the Marsh'**. At this time visiting companies to Margate included the Volkes family who were notable pantomime performers and long associated with the Theatre Royal Drury Lane pantomime. Also, the vehement J. H. Clines in a repertoire combining melodrama with Shakespeare. In 1886 the 'Marine Palace' was opened and was much akin to Music Hall and a rival to The Hall by the Sea, which went through a succession of different managements over seven years. Back at the Theatre Royal on September 25th Violet Van burgh made her début in a drama by Frank Harvey entitled, **'The Ring of Iron'**. She was tall, gracious and dignified and sought tutelage from Sarah Thorne. She married the actor Arthur Bouchier, who took the Garrick Theatre London where he played leading parts for some twenty years.

Queen Victoria's Golden Jubilee

June 21st 1887 was the celebration of fifty years of Queen Victoria's reign and everyone in Margate was invited to contribute to a fund to commemorate this. There was a parade of dignitaries through the streets, entertainment and jollification at the Hall by the Sea, children marching through the streets with a Cobb's Brewery commemorative medal and externally in front of the Theatre Royal, was a life-size picture of the monarch. Surprisingly an anniversary which had gone almost unnoticed was the centenary of the Theatre Royal itself. Sarah's younger brother Tom continued to come from London with the D'Oyly Carte Company and in addition to this was a piece from the Vaudeville Theatre, which was a successful adaptation by Robert Buchannan of Fielding's **'Tom Jones'**. Two of Sarah's other brothers, Fred and George, now also acted intermittently at the Theatre Royal. There was an E. Lyall a beginner as Othello and a Miss Ackroyd as Desdemona. Also, Sidney Valentine as Shylock, followed by a Nutcombe Gould in the same role and the Acting School continued to flourish. Now under the guidance of Sarah Thorne a new generation of players was entering playhouses in London and elsewhere. Another pupil Allan Aynesworth, remained in Margate for three years, later establishing himself as a West End favourite in the creation of the master comedy by Oscar Wilde of **'The Importance of Being Ernest'**. Also, Marion Lea, Florence Wood and Gertrude Kingston, the latter whom was to have her own 'Little Theatre' at the Adelphi London. In 1888 Violet Vanbrugh enacted Ophelia in Hamlet and Shakespeare continued in the fore in 1889 when the Vanburghs were teamed together in **'Much Ado About Nothing'**. Violet as Beatrice and Irene as Hero. Then, in 1891 with Evelyn Millard as Juliet and Richard Thorpe as Romeo and a young Granville-Barker as Paris. All three were destined to become famous especially Granville-

Barker with the early plays of George Bernard Shaw. Some other notable newcomers were Lennox Paul who was into farce and Ellen Terry's son, Gordon Craig seen as Charles Surface in **'School for Scandal'**. Some excellent touring companies continued between Easter and October when the Sarah Thorne Company might be performing elsewhere. Cleaning and repainting became a high priority as wear and tear had made its mark and in 1893 the Theatre Royal was again refurbished and re decorated. There was also a new 'Act-Drop' for the front of the stage which was a work of art for the audience to peruse between different presentations, replacing the previous advertising materials. Sarah Thorne was now acting less, other than in a role in which she was familiar and her main interest became the acting school as well as running the theatre. She never lost her perfect diction and always portrayed a believable version of the character she was playing. Her stock seasons were always good and visiting companies served to further enhance the reputation of the Theatre Royal. Even visits to neighbouring counties increased visitors coming to Margate as well as artists who sought to relax at the seaside as well as to perform.

Touring was sometimes a problem with dates especially in Chatham, so Sarah decided to take a lease on the Lecture Hall for seven years and renamed it **'The Opera House.'** This also prompted her to have a second home there as well encouraging the exchange of productions between Chatham and Margate which she undertook for several years. These exchanges were mainly confined to weeping dramas, costume comedies and farces and of course Shakespeare. D.H. Morrell and Frederick Mouillt had developed a strong partnership in the provinces and had successfully performed at the Theatre Royal Margate in Oscar Wilde's, **'A Woman of No Importance.'** They sought a seasonal allocation for this idea which was unfortunately unobtainable. The idea then arose of having a second venue in Margate and what about the ruin of the Assembly Rooms in Cecil Square. On the foundation of this ruin the partnership decided to build a bigger and more contemporary second theatre which would have a close proximity to the Theatre Royal and building commenced in 1897. Sarah Thorne was of course apprehensive about such a development as she continued her productions both at Chatham and at Margate and especially as the young Arthur Wontner had just joined her for what was to be the start of his long theatrical career. At this stage however, Sarah's health began to deteriorate due to a weakening heart. The new theatre designed by S. F. Davidson had a colonnade on Cecil Square and two others at Cecil Street. Inside was a colour scheme of creamy white pale red and blue tinged with gold. The proscenium opening was 31 feet wide and had a plush curtain of crimson and gold. The depth of the stage was 30 feet and the house had a capacity of 1,800 which was more than twice the capacity of the Theatre Royal. Application was made for a dramatic licence on July 11th 1898 which was granted and the **'New Grand'** as it was first known (later the **Hippodrome**) was opened on August 8th 1898. Whereas gas was still the main lighting at the Theatre Royal, at the New Grand it was electricity! On the opening night a comedian J. L. Toole took his place in the audience as he had retired from the stage and having become a resident of Margate. The opening production was the musical comedy **'The Shop Girl'** based on the book by H. J. Dam and music by Ivan Caryll and Lionel Monckton and a team from the **London Gaiety Theatre,** which was lavishly presented by one of George Edwardes companies. The well-known cast of the day were Stephen Adeson, Russell, Tom Fancourt, Topsy Sinden and Lillian Digges. How could Sarah Thorne at the Theatre Royal match this New Grand. Should she appear in her stand by, 'East Lynne?' Her supporters did rally round during her that week making large audiences indicating that Margate would not desert the theatre for 'newfangled musical comedy'. The Theatre Royal keeping to its planned schedule staged Henry Petticoat's drama, **'Hands Across the Sea'** to a full audience. It transpired that both rival theatres were playing to good houses until Christmas. Matinees were introduced at The Grand as they had been the growing trend in London and touring organisations visited with **'The Belle of New York', 'The Celestials,' 'The Geisha', 'La Poupee', 'The Circus Girl'** and **'The Gay Parisienne'**. Albert Chevalier of **'My Old Dutch'** fame was seen in his own play **'The Land of Nod'.** Notably the D'Oyly Carte Opera did desert the Theatre Royal for the larger stage of the Grand.

Nonetheless, the Theatre Royal continued with the stock company shared with Chatham and other strictly dramatic companies for productions of **'The Little Minister'** by James Barrie, **'The Liars'** of H. A. Jones, the melodrama **'Two Little Vagabonds'** and a stage version of the novel by Arthur Holmes-Gore of **'The Sorrows of Satan'**. Sarah Thorne's final performance was to be Parthenia in the second act of **'Ingomar'**, the tragedy of German origin. In 1899 came the twenty eighth and last of the travelling pantomimes which she sponsored. At this time Sarah's health was failing fast and she contracted influenza from which she took a bad turn and died at the age of only sixty-two on February 27th 1899, at her Chatham residence.

An Interview by A Sketch Newspaper Reporter on October 9th 1895

The purpose of the interview was to learn about the career of Sarah Thorne and as named by a Mr. Clement Scott, her 'Dramatic University'. Noteworthy points were that the little house in Hawley Square was a summer residence containing a pretty little drawing room prominently displaying souvenirs, the most memorable being a silver-mounted claret-jug, marking her contribution to a life dedicated to the theatre. Also, the influence she had in guiding and moulding the theatrical talent of the actors and actresses of her day. Of course, they felt a little apprehensive as she judged them, 'under the shelter of a little green baize screen' on the prompt side of the Theatre Royal Margate stage. At the time of this interview she was on the move to Chatham, where she had taken on a second theatre enabling her to have a viable theatre company for the whole year. Being so busy it seemed that it was never possible for her to take a holiday. Although her father had been the lessee of the Pavilion Theatre in Whitechapel she did not come from an acting family, although she had still a longing to appear in his pantomime. Having been allowed to play only for one night as a great treat it was on the understanding that she would never ask to act again, which she never did. She confessed however that she thought she had made quite a hit with this small part. A lesson which she passed onto her pupils, in that it is quite possible to do a great deal with very few lines. A point fully supported in the biographer's training and experience, in that on stage the last thing you do is speak. In Sarah's time acting schools did not exist but she acknowledged that the finest training she had obtained was in her early work with stock companies, observing the techniques of fellow actors. With her father, she actually had plays written around her by the stage manager who used to say 'I made her, sir!' She later went on tour to Surrey, Ryde, Dublin, Brighton, Glasgow and the St. James under Mrs John Wood's management.

Other Key Learning Points for Students of Stage Craft

Sarah Thorne advocated stock experience or 'learning through doing', as the best training, which was often very hard. It involved sometimes sitting up most of the previous night and in one case giving evidence in a trial scene on responses from the judge. She recalled an occasion when she could not remember when to answer 'yes' or 'no' to an enquiry and turned to a man nearby saying, 'Ask that man!' Apparently, it was this which gave her the idea of starting an acting school. Additionally, some newspaper reporters had mentioned the defective elocution of many London players, pointing out the need for a school of drama. In response to a question on 'What teaching method do you advocate?' Sarah Thorne's answer was to remark, have no method or rule, it is impossible! Each case must be dealt with according to its own needs, especially with absolute novices. I generally ask them to recite anything they know or read a piece of Shakespeare. Training usually begins with just walking on stage and speaking parts follow later when some capability can be identified. Not all pupils are novices and sometimes even old hands come to me for advice. My main objective is to bring out any latent talent, whilst taking care not to discourage any individuality. Hearing about the experiences of others can warn a beginner against faults and failings which they might take many years to find out themselves. The teacher should be without mannerisms which the learner might copy or imitate and even take from other students. It is so much easier to copy than to be original! Acting cannot most certainly be taught and what it essentially is, is the development of latent talent. I often have amusing excuses for failure such as an ill-fitting wig making an actor forget lines, or not impressing an audience. '

A week is often the longest time we have to rehearse but the same people do not always necessarily play the leading roles. I never promise anything and often change the cast at the last moment. London managers such as Sir Henry Irving and Mr Toole pay us visits and on one occasion Sir Henry remarked that the ladies were better than the gentlemen. I replied that 'I think the gentlemen's brains are so crammed with education, there is no room left for dramatic conception!'

List of Managers at the Theatre Royal Margate 1787–1965

1787–90	Mate, Robson and Booth	1866	Florence Webster
1790	Grubb and King	1867	Sarah Thorne
1792	Wilmott Wells	1873	Cathcart and Amory
1795	Shaw	1874	Robert Fort
1798	S. Russell	1875	H. E. Davis, Edward Price
1802	Robert Copland	1876	Frank Musgrave
1803	**Theatre used as auxiliary barracks**	1877	R. Fort (2nd Term)
1803	**Theatre used as auxiliary barracks**	1878	William Sidney
1804	Russell, Wilmot Wells	1879–99	Sarah Thorne (2nd Term)
1805	C. Didier	1900–05	Edmund McKnight
1807	Wilmot Wells	1905	H. E. Michael
1811	Robert Copland	1912	F. Weathersby
1814	Betterton	1915–29	**Theatre used as a warehouse**
1815	Egerton		
1820–40	E. F. Saville Faucit	1930	Wenter Charles
1841	**Theatre used as a Chapel**	1931	J Bainbridge
1842-43	J. D. Robson	1933	**Theatre used as a cinema**
1844	**Theatre Closed**	1933-34	C. Middleton
1845	Joseph Coombes	1934	Patricia Nye
1846	Miss Joyner	1937	Kelly and Cross
1847-9	T. S. Dowton	1938	R. O'Brien
1850	C. W. Gill	1940–48	**Theatre Closed**
1851–2	Edwin Holmes	1948	Crosse and Butler
1853–4	E. F. Saville Faucit (2nd)	1949	Will Hammer
1855	Richard Thorne	1950-3	L. Steinberg /T. Wyatt (Margate Rep)
1865	W. H. Swanborough	1954–56	Baxter Somerville
1956–60	**Margate Theatre Trust**		
1960–61	B. Somerville(2nd)		
1962–3	**Margate Stage Company**		
1964	D. P. Chaudhuri		
1965–68	Bland and Fogarty		

Period 1966 to 1988 saw various owners including Tam McKenna who ran a successful bingo hall and also carried out some restoration of the theatre itself. (Harry Jacobs 1978)

1988–1992 Jolyon Jackley
1992–2007 Michael Wheatley-Ward (General Manager Margate Theatre Royal Trust)

2007-12   Will Wollen
2007 onwards   Thanet District Council (TDC)

The Thorne Dynasty Key to Success

As can be seen from the list of managers, Edmund McKnight, who
was Sarah Thorne's son succeeded her for five further years until
1905, followed by E. Michael for six years and F. Weathersby until
the second year of the First World War when the theatre was then
closed for fourteen years until 1929. Short management periods
followed to 1940 when the theatre was closed during the Second
World War for a further eight years. Taking the period up to 1965
most serving managers had a maximum tenure of three or four years.
The exception is Saville Faucett, who had a twenty-year term
between 1820 and 1840. The longest periods of management were of
Richard Thorne and his daughter Sarah Thorne. Richard had been
trained in turn by his father and had ten children, all of whom were
actors at the Theatre Royal. He had an important network of talent
and experience to draw from on the London stage, which was taken
up by Sarah during her management years. Although competition
would follow later, especially from the cinema, this of course did not
apply in Sarah's time. The Theatre Royal became an institution
through Sarah's creation of her school of protégés becoming an
alumni to continue her vital formula for discipline and a professional
standard. An alumni of national stars which in turn assisted in the
survival of the Theatre Royal in spite of local competition from
other entertainments. Firstly, the touring circus of two sons of James
Sanger (who served in Nelson's navy), John and George Sanger.
James Sanger had been invalided out of the navy due to his injuries
and with the skills he had acquired from shipmates he undertook
peep shows and conjuring. Two of his ten children followed in their
father's footsteps and developed a circus empire. They had firm
foundations in Margate at the 'Hall by the Sea', which later became
the site for 'Dreamland'.

   A local resident of Margate, Tony Ovenden, from his research on
Victorian Margate cites a period of great prestige for the town
although with very similar challenges to today. A pattern of
bankruptcies, venues no longer fashionable and at that time the

threat of fire all extremely well researched in meticulous detail by **Malcolm Morely** in his book **'Margate and its Theatres'**.

In recent years however, Michael Wheatley-Ward (1992–2007), has had one of the longest terms of office as the Theatre Royal Margate's theatre director, second to Sarah Thorne.

At the corner of Cecil Square where the library and TDC offices now stand were firstly the eighteen century 'Assembly Rooms', burnt down in 1882 in the 'Great Fire of Margate', this site remaining

Hippodrome courtesy of margatelocalhistory.co.uk

derelict for fifteen years and being purchased by Morell and Mouillot who owned a number of theatres. In 1898 they opened what was called the **'New Grand Theatre'**, which in turn was to encourage the re-planning of Cecil Square. 'The New Grand' was purchased in 1905 by the South of England Hippodrome company and became known as the **'Hippodrome'**, which was very successful up to the First World War and considered to be a lovely theatre.

However, with the development of cinemas, it was converted in 1921 for the use of silent films accompanied by a full orchestra and until the Regal cinema in 1934 operating next door made it difficult to compete. Remaining closed during the Second World War and afterwards regarded as not viable as a dilapidated building. It was put up for sale in 1958 and bought by Margate Corporation in 1967 for £19,000 by auction and demolished as the site for the library and Thanet District Council Offices. Significantly, the Theatre Royal Margate is described by The Theatres Trust Guide for British Theatres 1750–1950 as of major significance.

As the second oldest in England, it still survives. Such an impressive Hippodrome became a cinema and in 1958 was demolished. The oldest theatre in England built between 1764 and 1766 is the **Bristol Old Vic.**

margatelocalhistory.co.uk

Reference

1. In 1827 the new **'Royal Pavilion Theatre'** opened at the corner of Whitechapel Road and Baker's Row (now Valance Road) with a production of *The Genii of the Thames*, initiating its famous nautical-themed productions, pitched at the local maritime community. It burnt down in 1856 and in 1858 was replaced with a theatre seating three thousand seven hu. A thousand more than Covent Garden! It became known as 'The Great Theatre of the Metropolis' and eventually in 1860, 'East London Opera House', with a wide repertoire including Shakespeare, opera, pantomime.

In 1874 it was again reconstructed by Jethro T. Robinson, a notable theatre architect who also designed two other East End theatres both of which are now lost, the **Grecian Theatre** in Shoreditch and **The Albion** in Poplar, which was oriental in style. It was this rebuilding of the Pavilion that included the construction of a new terrace on Baker's Row with interwoven Moorish arches, evoking the Alhambra.

2. Hall by the Sea Margate – In the amusement park opened in 1880 which became known as 'Dreamland' in 1920. The Hall by the Sea was a dance hall which was not a success.

3. Henry Irving – (1838–1905) To the disapproval of his stern Cornish Methodist relatives left a London Counting House for the stage in 1856. For ten years he was a busy provincial actor in Edinburgh and Manchester and had intense ambition. He acted for the first time with Ellen Terry in 1867. In 1871 he appeared as Mr Jingle in Albery's Pickwick and in the early 1880s changed the fortunes of the Lyceum Theatre with Leopold Lewis's version of Le Juif Polonaise named **'The Bells'.** 1878 he bought out Bateman's widow at the Lyceum with the idea of creating it as a temple of his art over a period of twenty years.

Chapter 5 – A Reflection on Events Contributing to the Re- Opening of the Theatre Royal Margate in December 1988.

Some Preliminary Questions

It is not intended in this chapter to give a compendium of the shows taking place during Michael's tenure as theatre director and those which are mentioned serve for illustration only. The biographer is once again extremely grateful to Ian Carter-Chapman for his scrapbooks of some of the news articles also referred to. However, the main focus is on administrative and management issues as a passage of key events, to provide an objective account intended to be of interest to any reader of this biography. Although, now in 2019 and some twelve years since the Theatre Royal was sold to the local authority, many unanswered questions still remain as to why this happened which will now be addressed. Questions arise as why after years of not wishing to know about the old theatre did the local authorities suddenly pump money back into it? Previously the Trustees had been denied proper brown road signs directing people to the theatre itself and now they suddenly appeared everywhere. It was no coincidence that in addition to the Theatre Royal seeking considerable investment at that same time, finance was also required for the Turner Centre in Margate and that the council went down the 'contemporary route' in order to gain the huge subsidy required to meet this new venture. Michael having been associated with the Turner Project since its conception had attended a private launch at an art gallery near Maidstone. It was proposed that as there was no museum for Kent, one might be sited in Thanet and art galleries to attract touring art shows, to give the whole project a viable edge with less dependence upon public funding. Consequently, when eventually it was decided to go one hundred percent down the contemporary art route, including free admissions, many were horrified at the huge public subsidy this would require. After the initial opening staging a Turner exhibition, the general consensus was that whilst it was pleasing to see more classical works in the gallery, this would not solely assist in the regeneration of Thanet. Perhaps lower local house prices and the high-speed rail link to London would be contributory factors at a later stage? Notable was the re-opening of the Ramsgate wartime tunnels which would draw in huge crowds. Significantly when the initial arts management took over the tenure from Michael Wheatley-Ward as Director of the Theatre Royal, why did this lead to the bankruptcy of the old trust? Apart from trading losses and the disappearance of the £60,000 endowment fund, why did the authorities not release into the public domain any accounts? Was it not coincidental that the authorities in Canterbury thought that when they closed their theatre for a two-year re-fit, the Theatre Royal might take some of their patrons on a permanent basis, which naturally is what they must have wanted to avoid?

How and why did Michael Wheatley-Ward, as a commercial theatre manager, come to be replaced at the Theatre Royal? By reading on, the reader will be presented with some more 'quizzical' questions.

Back to 1988

Early in that year Michael Wheatley-Ward had consulted the Estates Gazette and Jolyon Jackley, who was very keen to leave his current job, found out that the Theatre Royal Margate was at auction. This was because the bingo hall which had been operating in the building had gone bust and one of the mortgagees was selling it just to get their money back. Involved with all this was a local trust called the 'Margate Theatre Royal Trust'. Jolyon had found out not only the name of the solicitor, a James Robinson, but also the bank manager and had arranged an appointment for us all to go down about a week later to view the premises. So we hared off down there and got a key from the estate agent and walked into this old building devoid of functioning electricity. Jolyon whose father was the comedian Nat Jackley, remembered the Theatre Royal from his childhood days when he lived in Birchington. Jolyon had previously managed the Theatre Royal Windsor and according to an Isle of Thanet Gazette Article, regarded the Theatre Royal Margate as **'Windsor by the Sea'**. Whilst Jolyon was talking to the estate agent, Michael

Wheatley-Ward stood on that stage and looked out into the empty space and simply said 'Sarah Thorne, you have got to help, what are we going to do?' This of course being the Sarah Thorne previously detailed in chapter 4, who was the actor-manager at the Theatre Royal Margate between 1885 and 1899. Also, the founder of a 'School of Acting' regarded as Britain's first 'drama school' termed by Clement Scott, as her **'Dramatic University'**.

The auction was about to take place and Jolyon was so keen to buy it that he sent a cheque off for £100,000. However, the asking price was only £50,000 and Michael had said, 'This is silly but if you want to do it the cheque will bounce as there is no money in that account!' At the auction also present were representatives for the Theatres Trust Charing Cross Road London, as well as a representative from English Heritage. The auction started with an announcement that this was a theatre with a ghost and the bids went up one person having started at £10,000. When it got to £50,000 Jolyon stood up and said £100,000 and the gavel went down and he had bought it. Incidentally we had previously seen the local Thanet District Council, who stated that they could not help with the buying of this theatre, but if we bought it and sub-leased it back, they could get money to restore it through English Heritage. We returned at a later date to Margate, Jolyon having agreed even to sell his house with a facility from a bank in order to buy the theatre. One major surprise was that the deal with the Council had changed in that they could not help us buy it!

Consequently, there was no point in leasing it back and Jolyon was lumbered having now bought the theatre. Both John Muir the architect and I felt sorry for him although we were committed to help him, because having sold his house to pay for the building he now needed help in raising finances for maintenance and refurbishment. For the initial capital works, we went round various friends in the theatre business including theatre managers in London. Paul Goldsworthy who was manager of the Prince Edward Theatre, Stan Jarvis at the Globe Theatre (now the Gielgud, who had incidentally, also been the last manager of the Glasgow Empire) and between us we put up £20,000 worth of debenture stock, for which we became the directors of the Margate Theatre Royal Limited.

There were then some major problems. The building required urgent works and the architect advised us to apply for grants from English Heritage to cover structural issues in the building itself, including dry and wet rot in the timber frame. The re-licensing of the building through Thanet District Council was also a further hurdle, although none of this would deter Jolyon. He wanted to run it his own way and we couldn't prevent him, having also taken advice from a John Muir about how to get money from English Heritage. There were also problems dealing with Thanet District Council's Planning and Licensing Department and it seemed quite obvious that certain factors in Thanet did not want the Theatre Royal to be re-opened, having a preference for the Winter Gardens. Jolyon to give him his due decided to re-open that Christmas with a pantomime which was a decision taken in March for December 1988. Structural investigations into the theatre building had revealed water leaks, dry rot, wet rot and people had even previously let fire hoses off in the theatre.

None of this would deter Jolyon who was very admirable and Michael just felt that we had to keep the place going, come what may. Most formidable was the absence of a budget, since money which came in was immediately spent. This was a concern together with his single determination to get the theatre re-opened regardless. To raise additional funds we had tours, plus our own money as debenture stock and when he announced he was re-opening for the pantomime and he used the advances from the box office to pay for any bills. The Thanet Extra May 27th 1988 featured an article 'Out of the Dark', noting Jolyon Jackley for restoring the Theatre Royal Margate to its former glory. To present top class entertainment on a regular basis and enhance the cultural amenities of the area and therefore become a valuable asset. The Isle of Thanet Gazette on 22nd April 1988 featured an article on Jolyon Jackley's intentions to ' treat visitors like royalty!

The bank manager, a Bill Longley of Nat West, was a lovely guy and said that if he took charge of the building, the bank would loan an overdraft figure to help with re-building costs which, of course, would be continuous with extras such as re-wiring the place and getting the roof fixed at a very high cost, consuming more and more money very quickly. On a brighter and personal level for Michael, at this time an amazing incident happened on Saturday 17th September 1988.

I was sitting and worrying, as I normally did, and a lady walked by wearing a leather jacket, jeans and parrot earrings and said, 'Good morning, I'm one of the volunteers!' This was to be my future wife Terrie. Especially as I was thinking at this same time, 'Oh my God, I have lost all my investment here, but I have met someone!' We were engaged within the year then married and at the time of launching this book we will have celebrated our thirtieth or 'Pearl' wedding anniversary!

Back at the Theatre Royal we struggled on as the rehearsals started and even on the opening night we were still waiting for the licence to be issued by the council, which was a palaver in itself, but bless him, Jolyon got the theatre open for business at the eleventh hour. The audiences loved the pantomime which was really well put together and it took quite a bit of money but overall, we had a £17,000 loss, which we all felt was well worth the effort because it had enabled the re-establishment of this theatre.

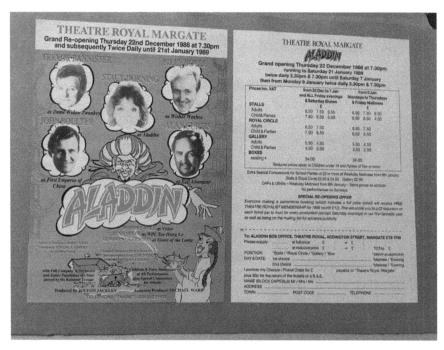

The Isle of Thanet Gazette on 16th December 1988 revealed that Jolyon Jackley's love of the stage had caused him to sell his house, to enable him to buy and refurbish the Theatre Royal, moving his wife and two young children to Thanet. That in just three months after gaining ownership he was also to appear on ITV's **'Stage-struck'**, with the full story in advance of the pantomime **Aladdin** opening in England's second oldest theatre and the first there for twenty-three years!

However, Jolyon had not thought what to do after this pantomime was over and the theatre was again dark with the crucial question, 'What are we going to do next?' The trust naturally agreed that we had got to put shows on and be a touring venue as well, which would require even more money. The bank loaned more and we booked some tours some of which were a bit shaky but they all took advance bookings which was encouraging. After the Aladdin's last performance we were offered for a now defunct pantomime set something like £10,000 but Jolyon wouldn't sell it. Michael recalled saying to him, 'You either sell, mate or I am resigning from the board.' Predictably he did not sell although I stayed on for a while longer until it was sold. We all had further disagreements and Jolyon decided that in the end he would continue on his own and we should all resign. So all the theatre managers who had contributed to the debenture stock decided to take a back step and just let Jolyon run it by himself. We could have pulled the rug from under him by fore closing the debenture stock which we did not want to do. Jolyon carried on for a couple more years under his sole management as the debts increased. He then started to put on plays which ran for three weeks which Michael advised should not be run for more than a few nights. Obviously, the pantomime was the one big event which could be depended upon to bring in money. A lot of mates in the business helped out but because of the debt load and other concomitant problems, eventually it meant having to go to court on these issues. He was in considerable difficulties and we tried to help him and had periodical meetings as debenture holders. One issue was to rent the theatre out to amateurs which came to nothing. It was all very interesting but also very sad, as I always had profound respect for him and defended him, primarily because of the way in the beginning the authorities had reneged on the theatre purchase. They of course might have had legitimate reasons for doing this but had provided no explanation whatsoever. Although the bank tried to save him, the court had to agree that the situation was untenable and that it was best if the theatre was closed down.

Ronnie Cox, who regarded herself as a lowly unpaid volunteer for sixteen years at the Theatre Royal, wanted the theatre to succeed although she acknowledged Jolyon as a man of firm conviction, who became bankrupt largely due to unpaid VAT. She felt so sad for his wife since he had originally pledged his house in order to purchase the theatre. She also recalled that the staff on the payroll always looked forward to Michael visiting from Windsor at the weekend, as they knew that they would be paid what was due to them. However, a rescue package was put together to help Jolyon in that the Margate Theatre's Royal Trust had raised money from the County Council and the Thanet District Council, amounting to £100,000 between them. It is remarkable that it was always £100,000, which comes up as a requirement for this theatre, to buy the theatre back from the bank and clear the liquidators, who had also had to find £100,000. The other £50,000 came from an endowment fund called the 'Castle Trust' which was based in Ramsgate and for which a Jimmy Robinson was also acting as a local solicitor.

It all got into a bit of a state when in basic terms the liquidator agreed to £100,000 for the freehold which was paid over and the Theatre Royal became fifty percent owned by the Margate Theatre Royal Trust and fifty percent by the Castle Trust. However, the major problem now was that both sets of trustees, perhaps due to communication problems, did not really get on. John Earl at the Theatre's Trust informed me that something had to done to re-open the theatre and get it going, since Jolyon had proved this possible. Michael happened to be in the office at the Theatres' Trust in London's Charing Cross Road seeing John Earl, who was retiring and looking for a replacement head of the Trust. Michael stated to him, 'Well I wouldn't mind going for that job'. John Earl replied, 'I've no doubt that you could do it, Michael, but I'd rather you take on rescuing your old theatre in Margate'. My ears pricked up when he said, 'We have got this problem with the two trusts which won't work together and we need someone we know who can do some head bashing!'

John Earl – Courtesy of Theatres Trust

So, as my wife Terrie had worked for Robinson Allfree (solicitors in Ramsgate and Broadstairs since 1897) and I knew Jimmy Robinson the solicitor, I asked for his help and he said, 'Leave this with me!' The next thing I knew was that I was on the train down to Margate and I was meeting with a Maureen Greig and Sheila Marshall, who ran the Margate Theatre Royal Trust, who were all equally worried about the situation because the lady who ran the other trust wasn't talking to them. I got very easily coerced into the trust firstly as a trustee, then as the Project Director for the Margate Theatre Royal Trust. This was a godsend because it was for me £10,000 per year on a part time basis. As for my shop in Windsor, the council had stupidly changed the one-way system the wrong way round and as a consequence of this we lost one third of our turnover. I looked upon it as the 'Good Lord helping out and said yes to the proposal of the Margatge Theatre Royal Trust. This meant that I spent the next few months commuting between the shop in Windsor and Margate, trying to get heads bashed together. I did actually meet the lady who ran the Castle Trust and I thought that we would get on however, for reasons best known to her she did not want to work with me. I advised the trustees that the only way we could keep public interest going and raise money for the theatre was to get it open as soon as possible, by creating a 'Friends Organisation'. We applied for a licence to do this in order to re-open but it was disallowed.

A very enterprising Thanet Officer said to me, 'Don't worry about this, Michael, form a club and they cannot stop you once you have a club licence!' We therefore were able to reopen and to give Thanet District Council its due they gave us the right advice on how to form such a club and to get the theatre up to a standard for the re-issuing of fire safety levels. The reopening production was a Music Hall by Gordon Clarkson, which captivated the public interest, with the proviso that you could only come in as audience if you were a member of the 'Friends,' as it was a private club. We raised money from various trusts and foundations to help towards re-equipping the theatre, because we had only had it sub-licensed firstly to open the stalls. Then as more money came in we re-opened the circle and finally the upper circle. To my complete and utter amazement, the accounts of the Margate Theatre Royal Trust actually showed that the theatre was becoming viable as it was making a working profit. However, there was a hell of lot of hard work going into it all and I had sold my house in Windsor by that time and had moved down to Ramsgate. Although living down here and working at the Theatre Royal I was still working two or three days per week at the shop in Windsor. I said to my dear old partner Gordon in Windsor, 'Gordon, I'll guarantee you two days off per week', with which he was happy and enabled us to keep the shop going. Not only did we rearrange the shop finances to keep us solvent, but I was also now down at the theatre keeping those finances going as well. One of the other interesting stories was that the trust often had cash-flow problems and I had to buy the bar stock for it from the housekeeping money that I owed Terrie my wife. I had to sell the stock in the theatre bar on a Saturday in order to go on a Sunday to get our food for the week!

Often Terrie used to say to me, 'Where's my housekeeping?' I would open up the boot and there would be beer and I would say, 'That's the housekeeping but we have got to sell it first!' I was also loaning the trust money to pay wages and I was building up what could be called a 'Loan Account' (financed of course due to the shop in Windsor). Every time we got grants in they would repay me so it was all quite legitimate although set up in a fairly crude accounts system for the trust. I always kept a watch on who we owed and what was coming in. There was a youth unemployment scheme enabling us to take on seventeen-year-old Jay Thomas who was a technician, which saved me a lot of problems backstage because I knew I had someone competent together with his dad Richard. Front of house we also had Ronnie Cox who was wonderful at running her team of volunteers which included a Julian Steel, who also became another life-long friend.

With Gordon Clarkson doing pantomimes we attracted more tours and overall the theatre was paying its way with the shows. Of course, constant repairs to the old building meant that we were also making losses so we decided to go for a lottery bid which was essential. I had met at an Art's Council function a fellow by the name of Brian Harris, whom I asked if he would help with the business plan. John Muir put the architecture plans together and the Arts Council said 'Yes.' The Theatres Trust in London put up 10% of £24,000 and the balance by the National Lottery who helped us to put this bid together and we spent an entire year on all this. However, the Blair government won the election and changed all the rules. I will never forget the day that a lady from the local Arts Board came down. Incidentally, you were not shown the letter they had received from the lottery as to why you failed with your bid, which was most odd. You were just told headings, such as the architecture plans weren't right and that there were joint ownership problems and some non-constructive comments. For example, I was told that I had used the wrong architect and I replied that he was being used by Andrew Lloyd Webber for restoring West End theatres so I didn't think he was that bad!

Then this woman said to me, 'Well, you've got the wrong business consultant', to which I replied, 'You recommended him to me! Which was true. They kept coming up with reasons why we had failed to obtain a lottery grant and I remember that when we were on stage this lady from the lottery looked at me and said, 'This is really why you have failed, Michael! When I asked, 'What do you mean?' Her reply was, 'You have failed to make provision to get someone in a wheelchair to the fly floor!' At that point, Michael Vickers who ran a local cinema, openly said, 'I have never heard such nonsense!' To which this lady replied, 'I really must take issue with that remark'. I stood there watching these two having a right old go at each another and thought, I had spent a year on this project costing £25,000, but it was worth every penny to see the ballet of action between those two. In reality the Theatre Royal had the oldest stage in the country and you couldn't alter it, with a staircase to get to the fly floor. Also, it was necessary to have a couple of strong men to pull the ropes to raise the scenery up and down.

Shortly afterwards I happened to privately complain about these remarks to the Lottery Advisory Director though I never got a conclusive answer, which revealed for me some of the possible short-comings of lottery support. In the meantime, our lady chair became ill and we had to find a new holder when fortunately, Elizabeth Gilmore, who ran the Ramsgate Festival stepped into this role. Sadly, after a year or two of trying to get finances back on stream with the aid of grants grant funding she died overnight. One of our new trustees Sir Alistair Hunter, was appointed as the chairman in 2000. Having taken over one of the first things he did was to get to grips with the Castle Trust, through the Charity Commissioners and to give the commissioners their due, as outlined in the official report dated 5th November 2002, they removed all the existing trustees for mismanagement and appointed a new set of trustees prior to the Trust being wound up and we then combined the two trusts. This brings us to 2001 when the trustees had the idea that they should get some permanent funding for the building by getting together with the Arts Council, which was a remarkable change of mind. Sir Alistair set out trying to get enough money out of local authorities in order to make the theatre sustainable, emphasising that during the previous ten years the Wheatley-Ward management had been attracting reasonable audiences. That such a historic theatre with heavy overheads needed a lot of financial support from local councils, if it was not to go under. He cited the Theatre Royal Winchester as having had £150,000 support. On reflection Sir Alistair had the difficulty of putting this message across to local councils who were perhaps looking for justification to their voters in social terms.

Sir Alistair notes over an eighteen-month period of this tactic was that the original narrative was undergoing a subtle change. 'You have got to support us properly to help our excellent team to keep the theatre going. This seemed uncomfortable for TDC and KCC because they thought that their voters preferred any money to be spent on social care, education and the police. Instead was a gradually looming counter message that the theatre had been badly run, was in financial difficulties and requiring the council to rescue it. Evidence was to be based upon a closer examination of the theatre's finances, with the view that the bar expenses were insufficiently controlled and that financial mismanagement, was to become the developing theme. In addition to this was that any package for change would require the departure of the current management of Michael Wheatley-Ward, who should be put immediately on 'gardening duties'. The trustees regarded this as grossly unfair and put up a prolonged resistance, which was also set to reduce Sir Alistair Hunter's credibility as far as TDC and KCC were concerned.

In 2003/4 we had a £90,000 a year package put together which was £90,000 from the Arts Council, £90,000 from Kent County Council and £90,000 from Thanet District Council over a three-year period, which meant £30,000 per year from each. The Arts Council to give them their due, put up the money and stated that they wanted us to put on some of their recommended productions, which presented no problems as far as we were concerned. We could still keep the commercial side and Kent County Council Deputy Leader was on our board and agreed that somehow, they would find their contribution. The previous Labour administration at Thanet District Council, had agreed £10,000 per year, but the new Tory administration would not increase it. So we were short of £20,000 or £60,000 over three years. The result was that we couldn't put into practice all the Arts Council's directives as we had to focus on being even more commercial. This meant tendering out for pantomime and all manner of things, including those which were not preferred. For example, we tried Pop Shows, Heavy Rock Music and T Rex, personally hated by the theatre management but justifiable from the money being taken in the bar and well worth it! The theatre was thriving and the graph was going up. We had a producer who came in for a year for the pantomime which did not seem to work well so Michael said to the board, 'I'll put my own one on in-house!' This we did and even I was amazed at the money we took going from a £20,000 per year pantomime to nearly £100,000. For the last year with Cinderella, we made a clear £45,000 profit. Those last two or three years at the Theatre Royal proved to be extremely memorable since the local operatic company was going under and we put on our own musicals. Don Gregory, who had been a Director with all the local groups as well as being Head of Drama at South Kent College, produced 'The Sound of Music', 'Calamity Jane' and 'My Fair Lady'.

We had an in-house amateur play-group, pop shows, pantomime, the Canterbury Festival and experimented with various shows. 'Waffle' reports from consultants were entirely irrelevant as a solution, although one had advised a reduction in the box office programme with a focus on having appeal to more outreach areas such as Cliftonville West and Margate Central, being the most 'deprived' wards, having a greater social appeal to TDC and KCC as a basis for a grant funding. By contrast this strategy was set not to please the Arts Council because we were not putting on primarily what they wanted, since we had no alternative in the absence of local council funding, thereby requiring a more commercial strategy for the theatre's continued survival. It seemed to Michael Wheatley-Ward that the key issues which led to the downfall of his tenure at the Theatre Royal was because we were annoying people by being so successful, regardless of the lack of public funding for the infrastructure of the building itself, requiring a capital investment fund for continuous maintenance. We also had to address the after effects of the lottery bid failure, although we had applied for a full licence.

One of the licensing officers came to see me at the theatre and said, 'Michael, can we have a chat because we have been getting a lot of complaints about the Theatre Royal' and I said, 'What sort of complaints?' He said, 'People can't get in because you are a club and we are now in a position to help you get a full licence.' This they did and the theatre graph started to go up further since there were no restrictions on audience numbers. The overarching problem was building maintenance, because we were re-investing working show profits on a continuous basis to restore the building itself on a new roof, new foyer, box office, carpets and toilet upgrades. Still not enough of course, because the theatre continuously needed more and more for ongoing building maintenance. On the plus side we were getting some very good stage equipment and modern lighting, but it seemed that anyone of influence who could knock us would do so.

Some Community Productions

In December 1997 Gordon Clarkson directed 'The Sleeping Beauty' with a local actress Mandy Simmons in the title role, Derek Tobias as Nurse Beecham, Heather Grant as Fairy Stardust, Joy Leonard as Fairy Carabosse and Simon Gregory as King Bertram. Gordon Clarkson who wrote the script also doubled as Maddles and the storyteller.

Aladdin New Year's Eve 1988 Left to right: Trudy Kingman, Robert Mill, Alan Curtis and dancers Trevor Bannister, Stacy Droning, Fiona McArthur, Gordon Clarkson, John Boulter, Jean Self, Linda Frith, Joanne Varley, Ian J Brown, Tara Redmond, Zoe Caryl

Derek Tobias as Abanazar in a later production of Aladdin

Anne Mickletwaite and Gordon Clarkson in Cinderella in December 1999

One day we had a last-minute visit from a lady from the Arts Council Area Board. She quite frankly went for me and Sir Alistair in such a way which even Alistair, as a diplomat, found most upsetting. Comments that really were not acceptable and he afterwards said to me, 'You kept your cool throughout that meeting' and I said, 'Well, I am used to them!' Apparently, this was a lady who was building herself up in the Arts Council to be the top dog and had obviously pushed people out of the way in the process, in terms which could be described as arrogant, callous and over-ambitious. The next thing that Michael as General Manager knew was that there was to be a series of meetings to which he was not allowed to attend, although he was on the board, which only the trustees were going to. He was kept informed however, by Alistair Hunter that they wanted to find a more permanent way of funding the theatre.

In the September of 2006 he received a phone call from a member of Kent County Council who said, 'Watch your back, Michael, we have been obliged to accept a deal from an Arts Official for the new Turner Centre and part of the deal is that the Theatre Royal has to go "more artistic" and you and Sir Alistair have got to go!' So some more consultants were brought in, allegedly at the suggestion of the manager at the Marlow Theatre Canterbury. These would be Arts Council consultants handling the Marlow's rebuilding programme, whom we had been informed were 'special consultants'. Significantly, no matter what we said they claimed it was worse, for example, 'You haven't got 30,000 patrons per year coming through your door yet.' 'Yes we have and it is already above that and at the end of the pantomime it will be higher'. Whatever we said was re-arranged and used by the local authority at a public meeting to make the case that we were heavily in debt, which we were not. We had £100,000 mortgaged from the bank in order to do building work and a £100,000 grant from equity trust fund which we never had to repay, unless we sold the theatre, because it was for building work backstage and the scenery dock. For accountancy purposes this was put down as 'debt' Some years earlier we had been advised by Jeff Fendall, a fundraiser, to have this written off but nothing had been done about it. So when it came to a big meeting of the council, they had put a package together to buy the theatre. The Kent County Council and Thanet County

Council had got together and said 'We will buy the theatre using grant money from a social fund', that they had discovered was available from central government. Alistair mentioned that in a heated conversation with the leader of the Council, it seemed they were over keen to get the matter out of the way before the end of the financial year. That money would be used to pay off the debt, but of course we did not have that much debt. Michael had put together a successful budget which had been backed by the bank; that if we increased our mortgage to whatever the new set figure might be, the interest on the loan would be payable by the friends, who were contributing about £12,000 per year. On the other hand, if we were to ditch everything other than commercial works the theatre could survive. However, this was thrown out by the Trustees who were under severe pressure to sell.

There was a full council meeting at Thanet District Council to buy the theatre and push it through and to this day I can remember the Chief Executive of the council saying, 'But there are more debts than you think with this Equity Debt of £100,000'. This was never properly explained and appeared to be a distortion of the truth. On the night of the council meeting I remember two clear points. Firstly, that only one Councillor, Chris Wells stood by me and the staff, albeit he had to vote with his party. Also, a mysterious thick mist appeared in the theatre and then just went, so was this an omen?

The result was that Sir Alistair had to tell me that in the sale package all the staff were being made redundant and the theatre was going to be closed for six months and when it re-opened, the Marlow at Canterbury would be running the box office. This of course did not endear me towards the manager of the Marlow. At that point the local papers told me they had had mail bags of complaints and I don't think to this day the council realised what they had actually done because there was a public uproar. After this event on conversation with Sir Alistair he revealed to me the tremendous pressure the trustees were under from the authorities to accept their non-commercial package. Also, on later reflection Sir Alistair considered that TDC ownership would mean that they could not ignore the Theatre Royal Margate in future. A situation which still prevails at the time of completing this biography in 2019. However, I decided that we were going to go in a gentlemanly fashion. Let them close down the theatre, but that I would hand over to whosoever and we wouldn't create a fuss. Actually, we wouldn't have been able to do anything else because it had been steam-rollered, consequently making me decide that the only option was an orderly retreat. We did this in such a way that David Rankin our masterful publicity manager, had redeemed that certain trustees who didn't want the sale to go ahead, had been virtually blackmailed in order to enable it to happen. However surprising and interesting things in the public domain, were revealing that we were actually doing better than anyone had acknowledged which was reflected in the Annual Accounts lodged at Companies House. Admissions had been going up, making the story not as black as it had been painted by the authorities, who it seemed had been so desperate to get the money to build an Art Gallery, that they just could not lose that opportunity. Perhaps they had been advised by the consultants that in order to stimulate the area, it was necessary to have a huge art project? In principle, I had not disagreed with the Turner Centre proposals in the beginning when it was first mooted, having attended a meeting where pictures by Turner were shown of the Margate of olden days. The presenters admitted that they didn't know what they were going to call it other than the 'Turner Project'. They were really keen to have a permanent museum for Kent based in Margate, with art galleries attached to handle all the artefacts as well as provide a commercial side to the income. This I did not totally understand but it seemed feasible and I backed it although I felt it was a loss leader, but which would bring people into the area. However, after having gone to the arts authorities of the day, they stated that it would have to be for contemporary art only. This was despite the existence already of an excellent 'semi commercial' contemporary art gallery in Ramsgate called 'Gallery IOTA' (Isle of Thanet Arts), run by a Philip Oldfield, which also did not get backing from the authorities and eventually closed down. Furthermore, as it was coming to the end of the financial year the head of the council demanded an immediate agreement of the whole project otherwise it would collapse entirely. My heart sank because I felt that an art gallery in Penzance might be alright but we were too close to London to make one in Margate feasible.

At a time when the whole country was getting lottery money for projects, some of which were going to be white elephants, were we really going to have another one in Margate? Well I didn't mind if it was going to be properly constructed but when they said that a deal had been done over us and that Sir Alistair and myself had upset people in the Arts Council, it seemed to me obvious that we had possibly been used as scapegoats. Reflecting after an interval of several years on these events which led to my departure from the Theatre Royal, I am conscious that this was fate as the Theatre Royal had really been in my life since I was but eleven. There was a terrible flood which had closed it once in 2002/3 and I certainly would not wish it to close down again or be demolished, as it could also be an excellent training ground for apprentices, postgraduate student actors, as well as for adult education programmes. Similar, in principle, to the re-incarnation of the New Theatre Royal Portsmouth

Perhaps these sad events were a reason at that time for me to step aside in order to gain a broader and more reflective view. Similarly, to the shop in Windsor when I used to stand at the wall on the opposite side of the road in order to gain the customer perspective. Important for me was that I had met many interesting people many of whom I would continue to remain in contact with. These included Keith Salberg a member of the Birmingham theatrical dynasty and Patrick Monkton a celebrated Hungarian actor, whose nickname for my wife and I was **'My liege and Mrs liege'.** Also, Jane Freeman and most of the cast of **'The Last of the Summer Wine'**. Through productions with Paul Harris came Mandy Winters and Suzanna Craft-Levine, a general arts practitioner, also doubled up as a full member of **'Lady Ratlings,'** one of the most prestigious charitable organisations, whose husband was a rabbi. I had also met some fascinating producers chiefly Jonny Mans and from across the pond on Broadway, Roy Somlyo, who had been David Merrick's right-hand man. It was during this phase that I helped kick-start the careers of Andrew Grays (my accountant's son now operating at the Guildhall Portsmouth), Lisa Payne, actress, Lydia Crosher, actress, Jo Pearson-Farr, actress and Ellen Gould, who was a natural comedienne. As well as on the technical front, Andrew Martyn and James Johnstone, who were both naturals in their field and inspirational in fostering the work ethic. It was also during my tenure that I increased my psychic powers, since according to my lady-friend Ann Belcher and Josephine Gottesville-Barber both mentioned previously as mediums, who told me that I was a carrier of spirits! This would explain that people very close to me such as my wife and Jay Thomas, who started with me as a sixteen-year-old technician, becoming in 2017 my executor and business partner. What was spooky was that if I'd be thinking of one of them they would phone me to say, 'Do you want me?' Another compelling aspect was the ghosts at the Theatre Royal Margate. After all, it is the second oldest theatre in England! (Chapter 6)

Reference:- The Grand Order of Lady Ratlings or GOLR is a prestigious charity within the world of entertainment founded in 1929 and a great honour to have bestowed. It is closely related to the Grand Order of Water Rats originating in 1889.

Chapter 6-

A theatre which harbours ghosts, potentially enhances its fascination, its enthralment and mystique. Although the subject of this biography has so far not admitted to experiencing paranormal occurrences personally, he does acknowledge the experiences of sightings reported by others. This chapter therefore seeks to consider this further. According to local reports, a progressive experience of hauntings began in 1918 when the ghost of the actress Sarah Thorne, (Chapter 4) was seen. A scream backstage which travelled across the stage itself and exited through the stage-door. A trapdoor leading to what was previously a 'smugglers' cave having a 'cold atmosphere' has been determined as an area of paranormal activity, backstage as well as on the stage itself. There have also been reports of scratching noises and voices and two shadowy figures alighting from the rear auditorium stalls to leave the theatre. W. J. MacQueen-Pope witnessed the appearance of a ghost in one of the private boxes who he believed to be the actor, who drew back the curtains and committed suicide by throwing himself from the box into the orchestra pit. This incident is believed to have happened during the late Georgian, or early Victorian period. One of the private boxes has been considered as haunted with a spirit creating strange lights that float around the stage area. It is thought that an actor who had played here was dismissed for some reason, bought a box the next evening and then committed this suicide.

During the first decade of the twentieth century the wraith of a man was seen sitting in the box so often that the management was obliged to permanently withdraw it from sale finally having it bricked up. Alfred Charles Tanner was interviewed about his sightings by Dr A. R. G. Owen, a distinguished parapsychologist as well as a Victor Sims in 1966. Tanner was working on the redecoration of the Theatre when he experienced some ghostly happenings. He had agreed to work during the night in order not to interrupt the day time bingo. On the first night there were no incidents but during the second he heard a series of sounds from the stage as if someone was whispering. Stopping to investigate he could find no reason for this and as he continued working as the floorboards began to creak together with the sound of footsteps just in front of the stage and moving towards him. Turning round to see who was there the footsteps stopped but nobody could be seen. Tanner heard the door of the box office bang violently although again no one could be seen. He then resumed his painting being entirely alone in the theatre, in the hope that the noises he had heard were 'natural.' Just as he had become calm again the phantom footsteps started again coming up behind him and halted. When he turned this time, Tanner heard a heavy thump on the floor between the front row and the stage.

Looking across the front of the auditorium, he swears that he saw dust rising, as if a real object had hit the carpet. Of course, there was no such object but could this be related to the suicide?

Working again on a third night he was again interrupted by a semi-transparent globular object about ten inches across, moving on the stage from left to right. The globe then formed the shape of a head before it disappeared through the exit door, the curtains having been opened by an unseen hand. On his next working night Tanner had an assistant Lawrence Rogers working with him. They both heard a curious bang from the dress circle and called the police, but no intruders were found. Dr A. R. C. G. Owen and Raymond Bayliss attribute the slow movement of the curtains bangs and footfalls, as set down by parapsychologists as typical of poltergeists. According to the theories of G. W. Lambert, some have said that the ghostly noises related to seismic disturbances. However, the question remains whether 'earthquakes' can cause localisation of such phenomena in the Theatre Royal Margate and can localised noises be confined to one position within a building? He conjectured that the ghosts at this theatre are best explained as poltergeists, with hallucination as a side effect in the case of the curtains and the 'face'. That the atmosphere of this theatre seems to be the most charged in England for psychic happenings. According to Raymond Lamont Brown, (1) Sarah Thorne came back to protest against the modern usage of theatre for bingo games.

Michael Wheatley-Ward now personally recalls that during the autumn of 2005 whilst showing a tour group round the theatre he witnessed a lady on her own downstage left, who was actually 'pushed' over the edge, causing her to break her leg in the fall. There had been no one near her but the indication was that as her back was arched, she must have been pushed by an unseen hand! A John Viger, who was the head of the tour group and a church conservationist, was amazed as to how this could happen.

At the full council meeting in the theatre in 2007, when the 'economies of truth' were presented to the delegates to get their votes to buy the Theatre Royal with public money, a mist slowly descended from the ceiling covering the inside of the theatre. Although it began to disappear very gradually, it was still lingering when Michael came out after this meeting had finished. Then on returning back afterwards it appears that no one was able to explain why or how this had happened. Some believe that there seems to be a curse on anyone who is non-supportive of the Theatre Royal.' Michael continued that, 'After I had been dismissed from the Theatre Royal, Jay Thomas asked me what I would like for Christmas and I said, well as you are back in the old theatre, can I ask for a private tour to see what they have done with the old place This was duly arranged the week before Christmas 2007.

As I wandered around the theatre as if on my original daily tour routine, I felt 'no spirits' and Jay confirmed the same. However, on New Year's Eve he phoned me to say that since I had been back in that theatre all manner of psychic phenomena had started happening, such as seats going up and down, lights going on and off and voices. On this I again consulted an Anne Belcher who was a medium, as to whether this would verify me as 'a carrier of spirits'.

Featured in 'Kent Life' December 2007 was a small article by Julie Deller entitled, 'A Case of the Wrong Ghost?' and raising several questions. For example, why were the lights in the foyer blazing long after being switched off? It also mentioned that during the 1930s the Psychical Research Society set out to investigate some reports about the theatre, Sarah Thorne being credited for any 'unusual happenings'. In 1955 the caretaker had reported that when he had turned off the gas bracket backstage, he had later found it to be on again so what explanation could there be for this? The Kent Life report also mentions an unfounded theory that violent emotions can also leave a lasting impression in the earth similar to electricity, arousing a brief re-enactment of an incident taking place in the past, even hundreds of years ago before the land was used for a building! Often experiences can never be understood and are unexpected. Julie Deller also mentions any receivers of happenings as having no fear but felt themselves to be in the presence of someone, although they were unable to relate whether it was a man or woman. Gordon Crier producer of the BBC 'Band Waggon' recalled that during his acting days at the Theatre Royal in the late 1930s, Sarah Thorne would be 'watching' the matinee from the stage box which for fire reasons had been bricked up so she had to watch it from the wings behind a baize screen.

Some Experiences in Some Other Theatres

Richard Jones, a London guide, has written a number of books on haunted places, one entitled **'London's Haunted Theatres'**. Here are the alleged experiences witnessed by individuals as well as groups of people either collectively or at different times. This chapter also explores some hauntings which Richard as a 'Blue badge' London Guide has quoted on websites such as HYPERLINK "http://www.londonparanormal.com/theatres"www.londonparanorm al.com/theatres As well as https:/www.spotlight.com/news/archive /2013, also accessed for this information.

Adelphi Theatre

A great actor William Terriss is said to haunt here, having died in the arms of his lover after being stabbed to death at the stage door in 1897 by a jealous bit part actor who was found to be insane. In 'Haunted West End Theatres' by Ian Shillito and Becky Walsh this was mentioned except that the name of this actor was a Richard Prince, convinced that William Terriss's talent had kept him out of work for ten years. Terriss is also said to haunt the Lyceum Theatre as well as Covent Garden Tube Station. It has also been reported that the previous day before the murder his understudy in a dream had a vision of Terriss lying on the dressing room steps with blood flowing from a wound in his chest.

Dominion Theatre

In 1814 this was the Horse Shoe Brewery, when a large vat containing a million pints of beer which was ruptured and flooded the area killing eight people in the 'London Beer Flood'. Several audience members have reported seeing a fourteen-year-old brewery worker Eleanor Cooper in the theatre and a child giggling as well as poltergeist activity.

Her Majesty's Theatre's

The actor-manager Sir Herbert Beerbohm-Tree is alleged to have made several appearances on stage here at his chosen spot to watch performances from the top box and stage right is where his ghost has reportedly been seen. Some occupants of this box have reported 'cold spots' and as well as it opening suddenly. In the 1970s production of **'Cause Celebre'**, the entire cast watched the ghost walk across the theatre at the back of the stalls.

Theatre Royal Drury Lane

The Theatres Trust mentions that the original theatre was built on this site in 1663 and destroyed by fire 1672. The second which opened in the presence of Charles II in 1674 was re-built by Sir Christopher Wren. However, it was eventually to be considered too small and out of date and consequently it was demolished in 1791. A third theatre designed by Harry Holland was opened in 1794, but burnt down in 1809. The fourth and current building was designed by Benjamin Watt and opened in 1812. Because of the longevity of this theatre it is alleged to have had many ghosts. A Joseph Grimaldi had a distinguished acting career and laid the foundations of pantomime here. He portrayed the character of a white-faced innocent rogue which looked like a clown, which to this day are still known as 'Joeys'. The demands of his craft led him to a crippling disease which forced him to give up acting altogether. He became destitute and a benefit performance was set up for him in 1818. He had to be carried onto the stage where he performed seated having lost none of his magic. He died in 1837 and his ghost has returned many times with the administration of a mischievous kick of which actors, cleaners and usherettes have experienced. Dan Leno famed for clog dancing and portraying a pantomime dame, suffered badly from incontinence. He used perfume to disguise it and some have experienced his presence by the smell of lavender. Apart from this, actors have reported being tugged from behind. Some passing the dressing room that was Leno's have reported a rhythmic drumming sound as a rehearsing of his famous clog dancing routines. Then the 'Man in Grey' who appears in the daytime from one side of the upper circle crossing to the other side and disappearing into the wall. This apparition was witnessed by the whole cast of 'The Dancing Years' by Ivor Novello, in 1939 as they were all on-stage for their photo call. He has also been seen by firemen, theatre managers and other staff as well and sometimes sitting in the end seat of the fourth row by the central gangway. What was unclear was the purpose of this apparition until the wall he disappeared into revealed a hidden room behind it, in which there was a skeleton with a dagger protruding from its rib cage and surrounded with remnants of grey cloth. Speculation was that as a young man in the reign of Queen Anne (1702–1714 daughter of James II) came to London, having gained the affections of an actress at this theatre and was murdered in a jealous rage, by her actor lover. The body had been placed in the hidden recess and lay undiscovered until the Victorian renovation of this theatre. The ghost of the man in grey however is very welcome one, because he only seems to appear at the beginning of a successful run at this theatre and his antics have been to push performers to positions where they can best deliver their lines.

Piccadilly Theatre

The theatre is said to be haunted by Evelyn Laye who starred in the opening production in 1928. She died in 1996 and her photo which hung in the theatre's offices was moved. Apparently, the poltergeist became especially violent until the picture was returned and everything went quiet once more.

The London Coliseum

One subaltern a junior officer in 1918 made his last visit before going to the Western Front. He was killed and his mortal body lay in Flanders mud. However, on October 3rd 1918 his ghost was seen in the theatre as he slowly made his way down the rows of the Dress Circle and only minutes before the dimming of the house lights, he took his seat two rows from the front. An Emma Martin confirmed that on the 19th October she saw the same figure and on concentrating on the production, she found that it gradually disappeared.

The Old Vic

An actress, even in death, continues to act as if in her final scene.

Theatre Royal Haymarket

Dame Judi Dench is reported to have seen the ghost of John Buckstone who was Actor-Manager in this theatre in the mid-1800s. Apparently considered a 'friendly' phantom, he is heard reciting lines in Dressing Room 1 and sometimes appearing in the Royal Box, in stairwells and even onstage during performance.

Theatre Royal Stratford East

During Michael Wheatley-Ward's first job at this theatre the barman told him about Fred Fredericks, the second owner, who was said to haunt this theatre. One night, hearing movement in the Upper Circle this barman fired a prop gun from the stage at the noise and it all went quiet. Next morning a cleaner said there was blood on the Upper Circle floor but how true this was he does not know. (According to 'Wikipedia' Freddie Fredericks is thought to walk its dark corridors still, reported as a small tubby fellow dressed in brown, said to be friendly and comes to see his initials FF, in the middle of the arch spanning the stage.) This is also illustrated in London's Haunted Theatre Land from:' Phantoms of the Theatre' Satellite Books 1977 by Raymond Lamont Brown).

Wyndham's Theatre

Opened in 1899 and managed by Sir Charles Wyndham whose grey-haired ghost has been reported lurking near dressing rooms.

Theatre Royal Portsmouth

Appearing in the Portsmouth Evening News on Friday October 4th 1957 was a report that then manager Michael Wide, considered the Theatre Royal haunted. After sleeping over several months in a dressing room he became aware of two ghosts, one whom he believed to be the theatre's founder, Henry Rutley. I walk along the corridor to my office, I sometimes have a feeling of friendship as if I were being patted on the back, with the words, "That's the stuff, old boy!" There was a haunted room next to his because on returning back one night he saw a light on in that room, but walking in to switch it off gave him a very 'creepy feeling'. Exactly one hundred years after the theatre's opening in 1856 a chorus girl returning to the Rutland Room on the third floor found that it would not open. After going for assistance no key would open it. However, firemen breaking in found that it had been unlocked all the time.

Reflecting back on his years at the Theatre Royal Margate Michael Wheatley-Ward knew that the professional standards he achieved there were essential to maintain at any future venue in which he might be involved. For instance, some non-professional companies had initially stated that they could not afford the rent, although in his view this was quite reasonable. So as Theatre Director he had to prove to them that non-professional productions could still pay this rent. He recalled a series of musicals starting with **'Oklahoma!'** followed by **'Hello Dolly'**, which were all done within budget. Then three large productions, **'The Sound of Music'**, **'Calamity Jane'** and **'My Fair Lady'**, all with Don Gregory, who was a senior lecturer at Folkestone College who also ran his own amateur company – 'South Kent Theatre'. He was very experienced and brought a professional touch to the musicals. These shows actually took more money than ever before covering the production costs as well as the rent for the theatre for the show week. Although 'Hello Dolly' actually did lose some money, mainly due to problems with the set and having too large an orchestra, this experience was set to improve the costing projections for future shows and in particular plays, which had been initially considered by some as too expensive to undertake. **'The Farndale Avenue Housing Estate Townswomen's Guild Dramatic Society - Murder Mystery'** comedy, involving all the staff, was a substitute production due to a let down that week over the cancellation of an amateur booking in order to bridge that gap and it worked. On further analysis, all the productions particularly the pantomime seemed to yield no more than an 'x' or a static box office figure. Initially the board had told Michael to tender the pantomime out which he did, although later problems led to them to reverse this decision and agree to an in-house pantomime that was less costly. Again, he remembered being quite amazed in 2001, 'When we put this on with a local radio celebrity and the static box office takings shot up.' This would be the reinforcement for the policy for doing our own in-house productions. Michael recalled that he had restricted the pantomime to no more than two hours including

148

intervals, with emphasis on more comedy, making it a fast-moving experience which was a formula for success. Then I was introduced to a director who already had a cast, he introduced me to a chap called Robert Meadwell and a production of **'Dick Whittington'**. This came about as a result of a change to a prior agreement with the Marlow to do Cinderella at the Theatre Royal having been breached, resulting in a production of Dick Whittington as a substitute. More significantly, I could not believe the turnover as the box office bookings continued to increase, partly due to our on-going monitoring of the reasons for our audience demand. Together with a highly supportive local press, the artists themselves and most importantly, the theatre staff who related audience feedback to me, which I probably would not have ever seen or heard of backstage. This included some of the antics, such as, 'This guy is not doing this right!' Nonetheless, all very important feedback in order to acquire the overall view of a production from an audience perspective and developed through a continuous 'noises off' monitoring process.

A further innovative development that occurred purely by accident was a Greek tragedy company called 'Actors of Dionysus'. They were desperate for a date for a type of play I had never tried before in Thanet, but it was later revealed as being on the curriculum for the 'Open University'. This production filled the place and most importantly, the Actors of Dionysus (God of wine and ecstasy) afterwards became regular performers. I did also try a number of artworks brought from the fringe in London, one or two of which constantly lost money, although they were financed by the Arts Council and for which bad comments were received from audiences, so I ceased to do them. Vital feedback obtained through networking the audience and 'ear-wigging' conversations, or by just going round and asking people 'What did you think of the show tonight?' I am a firm believer in this as a practice which I still carry out at the Sarah Thorne Theatre, Broadstairs to this day. Asking straight questions such as 'Did you like it?' Sometimes receiving such responses as 'It was too bloody loud!' Consequently, I set out to gain an honest perspective from an audience as a means of putting on what people actually want to see. Of course, you have to have the guts to experiment and put on the occasional thing to test the water, such as in the case of Actors of Dionysus and similarly when we tried comedy. I was amazed that comedy costs even more money because of the comedians' fees, but if you did very well in the bar, together with the box office takings these costs could also be met. I am currently considering this approach for the Sarah Thorne as well as fund-raising, as I will have to pay £100 per comedian. The vital question is will we be able to sell enough tickets which of course is always a gamble. Important to remember is that if you aren't prepared to experiment you don't get anywhere. I did this all the time at the Theatre Royal and would also sit through works in rehearsal as well. It always annoys me that a lot of theatre bookers and publicity managers never do this, in order to assess what they have been publicising and I don't know why this should be. My mentor Sir Oswald Stoll used to sit in the box at the London Coliseum and watch every variety act, making notes and consequently I have followed his example. If you don't see it yourself then how do you know what went wrong or right and how can you make a judgement? This simple strategy must in my view, always be part of the job and an objective criticism is much more informative as feedback than a subjective one, based merely on a personal opinion. It was this kind of first-hand information which I am sure helped me to have an overall successful tenure at the Theatre Royal Margate. Of course, I also had a lot of very good staff with commitment who could always be trusted. I always listened to them and after all they were all volunteers until we got further funding, enabling them to be given a small remuneration for their services.

I didn't have a totally free hand, as I was subjected to a Board of Trustees as well as a management committee to be challenged for finance. I did however persuade them to go from a manual booking system to a computerised one, initially perhaps because we had caught one of the 'Friends' with his fingers in the till! A practice of which we are all aware and which is not uncommon. The people operating the bar were also volunteers and so were the ushers and programme sellers. To encourage good-will we gave them a free drink or an ice cream each night for being there.

Theatre Royal Birthday Cake

I remember that one volunteer had parked his car in the wrong spot and got a £20 fine, which I paid because I did not want him to be out of pocket. The office staff, including the box office manager, were all paid and any additional staff, as and when we could afford them. We sought all age groups to be ushers and it is ironical that they were more elderly than young. One youth came in with studs in his lips and I pointed out to him that this would be difficult for older audience members to accept and he removed them. He was not a drama student but just wanted to go into the theatre which a lot of them think they can do and of course they all want to be stars and go to the top of the business, having no concept of the amount of work involved. During my tenure at the Theatre Royal I got married to Terrie who was always very supportive with everything I tried to do.

Mentioned in Chapter 5, was that at the end of my time at the Theatre Royal myself and the staff were going to go in a gentlemanly fashion, handing it over to whoever was to take over. David Rankin had always done a masterful job in redeeming into the public domain documents which may have been covered up or even lost. Needless to say, that those last few weeks in harness were to be a testing and important period for the future of my life. I thought that it was important for me to see the leader of the council, in order to point out a few home truths over what had actually been going on business-wise and who even agreed to come for coffee, which I thought was very magnanimous of him, since they had the whip hand. However, I got a clear indication that perhaps he was the mouthpiece of the council and not the one firing the shots. When I handed him all the correct financial information the answer was, 'Well, this has to go to other people to be analysed!' It seemed to me he was actually realising that a lot of what he had been told was not correct, but being a good politician, he had to be careful what he said. He remarked, 'Oh, there might be room for a compromise!' However, I knew that by now we were too far down the line to reverse the decision about the future of the theatre. Also remarkable was that they had actually appointed an interim manager to take over from me before they actually told me officially, which was one of the grounds for my redundancy claim. I was also conscious that of the interim managers selected by the trustees the first, on gaining a full explanation of what was happening, had declined the post and this also applied in the case of the second choice! The third was therefore a 'bottom of the list person', for when I met him the impression was that he seemed good at giving orders, although he could not actually do the job himself. When things were explained to him it appeared that he would normally have passed this information on to someone else, rather than make a decision himself. For example, he had no idea of modern computerised accounts and although I am not an expert in this field, I understand the concept of what is actually required. However, he clearly had no idea of the processes involved in a computerised box office system and all the staff were coming to me and saying that for an interim manager, he didn't know what time of the day it was! It was unsurprising to all of us therefore that Thanet District Council had had to sack him. I remember the last day of the handover which for me I found a little hurtful in that they wanted to copy everything on our computers in case we didn't leave them in the correct fashion. I left all my reports of the pantomime turnover and everything that was important to be passed on to the next manager. In fact, it was noted by a council official that we had left the theatre in a very good state. However, there seemed to be an underlying feeling that they just did not trust us and, in some respects, I can't say that I blame them, although this atmosphere made things a lot more difficult.

Theatre Royal Open Day for the Lottery

The day that I was actually to leave, this interim manager got all my keys and put them in a plastic bag which was put to one side in the office. Then all the locks on the doors were changed and we were out. In my opinion this handover did not have to be undertaken in such a callous fashion, but I did upset this new appointee as they were changing the locks when I said, 'I know two ways of getting into this theatre without upsetting the alarm system, but I am not going to tell you!' When the final week had arrived, the press was unprecedented in that all the shows were sold out, including 'The Big Ballet' and Marty Wilde. Ann Widdecombe came down to do a fund-raiser for the local Conservatives, ironically, whose hierarchy had caused all these problems, but she was also a complete sell-out. We ended with 'The Gang Show' which we had founded at the

Theatre Royal and on handing in the keys we then got our redundancy cheques and consequently I now felt a great void in my life. It has to be remembered that over the years I had loaned and been repaid a lot of my personal money, used to keep the theatre open, due to the absence of available financing and as an alternative to the Arts Council route, with its tendency to support non-commercial projects at that time. That retrospectively this had all proved to be worthwhile since the theatre operations had been successfully run, disregarding building maintenance requiring continuous capital investment (Chapter 5). Although I was still on speaking terms with the trustees I now felt in a totally vacuous state.

Our friend David Languish who was both a friend of Kenneth Williams and Judi Dench was staying with us for a week, for which I was grateful because prior to this we had been working flat out for months in order to ensure that the handover would be conducted smoothly without any problems. On my first day of redundancy I started to sort out my personal affairs having received my cheque, although not for the correct amount. I had only been on the actual payroll for ten of my nineteen years. Prior to this I had been considered as self-employed and charging the trust on a 'Contract of Services' basis, as we all did. We had never been on the actual payroll itself until the last few years. Consequently, I got barely half a year's standard salary but the chairman said to me 'fight it!' and this I did. Before we actually left the theatre all the staff had agreed to have a collective meeting to decide just how we were to go about claiming our legal rights. This subsequently meant seeking the services of a solicitor to start the proceedings and in the meantime, not cash our cheques, since this would imply that we had accepted the first deal. However, once everything had been put in motion we were to settle out of court, gaining a little more all-round which in reality, turned out to be what we should have got anyway. If we had actually gone to court, we would have lost everything and of course there would be the legal costs to be met as well. We were advised by several people, including my wife Terrie's legal friends, that we had obtained the best deal. There was one member of staff who had said no to the deal and we had to persuade her that if she did not accept it, then we would all lose out. One of the trustees stated that they would not have objected to me having further money, but I thought it only fair that the staff should get their justifiable amounts based upon their years of service. I was aware that as I did not wish to be singled out in this way as this determined the final outcome.

My First Experience of Redundancy

As I had now closed the shop in Windsor and was operating a part-time mail-order business, for the first time in my life since my days as a sixteen-year-old at the Theatre Royal Stratford East, I was actually out of work. I thought therefore, 'What shall I do?' I was advised to go to the social security people to register my national insurance number in order to get it credited. This involved going through all the razzmatazz of responding to questions in what was a simple case. Although redundant I had enough money to live on for a year and was told 'We'll credit your national insurance but you won't get a penny!' which actually, I did not expect. So for a year I was to go through this procedure of signing on every two weeks, saying that I was looking for jobs which I was, whilst trying to decide what I should do next. Of course, I also had to give evidence that I was doing this. Significantly what I encountered was 'ageism,' in that I was perceived as not the average employee and would probably try and take over the firm, being the age of fifty-seven with all my business experience. I was offered jobs through contacts in London including managing West End theatres and working for other producers. However, I felt that I could not easily leave Thanet as I had now put my roots down in Ramsgate. I did have a magical call from Michael Friend my partner in summer seasons basically saying, 'What the hell are you going to do, you cannot just sit at home doing nothing!' To which I replied, 'No, it is too late to do the summer season this year, but I think we could look around for somewhere to do it next year.' He said, 'Great, let's work to that', which is where an idea of seeking out another theatre came about. At the same time as this I had a bit of luck enabling my continued economic survival, in that because I had registered 'unemployed,' I had a 'Loss of Income Insurance' which was activated, paying out further money. I then completed a cash flow statement on how I could survive if I was living on the state pension and thought, well you might as well get used to it now than wait until later. So I worked out such a cash flow assuming I had no income at all for four years by re-arranging the mortgage and the money we had and my lump sum, which I was expecting to get from the pension fund on reaching sixty. I clearly remember a week before the financial crash in 2008, having had a premonition that it was about to happen. Consequently, I sold all our personal investments which reduced our risk, enabling me to have extra cash to live on in the meantime. I elongated this period right up to January 2015 on reaching sixty-five and in receipt of the state pension as well. I concluded that I could survive and even if I didn't get a theatre site then we didn't have to worry about my income for the first year or so. Additionally, of course there was Terrie's income as well. The insurance company queried what the business in Windsor actually was and I told them that I was paying off a bank loan by buying and selling online. On this they seemed quite happy as I was not paying a Class A stamp on any earnings.

On reflection of this experience I was conscious that there were quite a lot of anomalies with the social security system and felt strongly enough to write to both our MP for Thanet South at the time, Laura Sandys and Frank Field, a Labour MP. We had fallen on hard times but weren't allowed to get anything at all from Social Security which we had paid into and a lot of people got, having put in nothing and surely this had got to change? One of the most interesting things about my redundancy was that it proved who my real friends were. I am thinking of both Jo Tuffs and of the Broadstairs Folk Festival and Rosie Turner of the Canterbury Festival, both of whom took me out for lunch and treated me with kindness. There was even a couple of people whom I thought that I had fallen out with because I had to be tough on business at the Theatre Royal, who actually wrote to the press condemning the authority's actions. The headmistress of the school where I was a governor, Cathy Smith and her fiancé, together with my wife and I had developed a very close friendship as she had had a difficult time with the authorities over the school amalgamation. So much so that when she married her fiancé Nick, she asked me to give her away at the wedding and my wife Terrie was the 'best man!' This episode was very unnerving for the Catholic priest undertaking his first marriage ceremony. All these kind people helped me to undertake the first days of unemployment in my entire life, which fortunately was not to be for long.

The Search for New Theatre Venues

I looked at various buildings in the Thanet area for possible theatre sites, such as Birchington's Village Hall and the old Motor Museum, which was in a dodgy state and my architect had said, 'Do not touch this with a barge pole', as well as local schools. My friend Richard Thomas said, 'Have you been into the Hilderstone Centre yet?' I said, 'No, but it is on my list'. I walked in and made an appointment for a meeting with the Head of Adult Education and as the manager showed me round the Hilderstone I just could not believe what I was seeing. Here was a very simply equipped standard theatre that had been closed as a result of losing its licence. They pointed out (which to me was a red rag to a bull) that they had had the Arts Council in there putting on 'wacky' stuff and it had lost the audience. So I said, 'Well, I can have a go at putting theatre events on here such as a Summer Season Rep, what days of the week can you allow me to use it?' They informed me that this could only be on Saturday and Sunday afternoons and evenings, because for the rest of the time it is used by Adult Education and also Hilderstone College. As there was no licence I thought it would have to be a club one, which of course took me back twenty years previously at the Theatre Royal Margate, where I had a building which wasn't being used properly and no licence. I perceived this therefore as a re-run of a previous time or déjà vu. On returning home I wondered what I should call this new ventire. On my desk upstairs was a picture of Auntie Pat Whitcombe, who was Jolyon Jackly's aunt by marriage and whose ashes are interred in the wall at the Theatre Royal Margate. No lies but I looked at the picture and said, 'Auntie Pat, what am I to call this new venture?' Back came the words 'Sarah Thorne'.

Thinking that it would be megalomanical of me to undertake this new venture on my own and for nothing, I asked my former volunteer staff at the Theatre Royal whether they would want to join me and they all said 'Yes'. Mainly because we all felt we did know how to run a theatre and felt cheated by the authorities and wanted to drive that point home. Much relieved I said well, 'There won't be any money in it but at least we can prove to people that we know what we are doing!' I let Gordon Eyles continue with the finances and David Rankin, although he was looking for a job said he would do the publicity and the box office and Jay and his Dad would be the technical support. I also went round my producer friends who had had to cancel their shows with the Theatre Royal and I said, 'Have you got any dates for this autumn for your plays?' Michael Friend was doing 'Mrs Warren's Profession and John Goodrum was touring 'The Ripper Files and the dear old Channel Theatre were doing 'The Ragged Trouser Philanthropists' (based on a book by Robert Tressell about a group of working men who are joined by Owen, a Journeyman and philanthropist who rouses them to have a view of what is a just society). We had left Margate in April 2007 but by the end of May I had not only found a theatre, but had booked in shows commencing from 29th September and this gave us the run up to Christmas on the basis of one show every three weeks.

Putting the Sarah Thorne Theatre on the Map

The next thing was to let people know what we were up to, so we did a press release. Although we were to charge £15 per year to be a friend, I was amazed that cheques just flew in. We had a phone call from Adult Education saying we know you are not taking over the theatre until September but there is post arriving already! We decided on an opening day for the box office in August and I had the lovely task of receiving cheques galore including £100 from the Friend family, who owned Northdown Farm and all in all we had £2,000 in the bank account. The press loved the story and of course I was still on the roll for what had happened at the Theatre Royal. On September 29th on the opening night we played to about 100 people, including the ex-chair of the council Geoffrey Kirkpatrick, with all the regulars and it was a successful evening. Whilst all this was going on the council had got rid of their interim manager at the Theatre Royal who was proven to be useless and had replaced him with a member of the council staff as an another interim measure, to take over the job until they appointed a permanent Artistic Director. Apparently, they had spent all the money from the sale of the theatre in refurbishing it but in such a way that I could not believe. They had followed the designs for the new toilets in what was known as the 'Old House', but had removed all the interior picture gallery which we had put up, depicting the old days of the theatre dating back to the late 1700s. They had done this in order to remove the wallpaper which they didn't want and also had changed the colour scheme. It was beige rather than dark carpet in the dressing rooms so that it looked very nice and 'arty'. They had removed anything which was an obvious sign of 'commercialism'.

For instance, in the Dress Circle, there was a ledge on which to put tickets and ice cream which had been removed. The bars that we had decorated were never put back being presumably not up to their standards. Instead they put in totally impractical marble or stone counters, as glasses could easily be broken and the whole thing in my view, demonstrated a complete waste of money. What they did not do which I had asked for in my report, was to renew the boiler that was much too heavy on gas consumption, as well as the seating and carpets that were also in need of modernisation. On going back for a private visit at Christmas I thought where have they spent the money, certainly not in the places where it was required? The Theatre Royal Margate Trust had sold the theatre to the council for I believe £300,000, who had leased it back to the trust for which they now paid a rental. They had of course started to use this liquidity exchanged in order to refurbish as well as pay off the old staff and make new appointments. They appointed Will Woollen as Artistic Director and ironically, our very own Jay as a technician after an interval of six months, which was the legal requirement for his acceptability to be re-employed with them. I was of course pleased that Jay had returned because he was able to tell me the details of what had happened since I left. A lot of what we had on our 'Programme of Works Schedule,' was not undertaken at all and what had been done seemed to be in order to create an 'arty' effect. Within a few weeks of his appointment I was to have a conversation with Will Woollen, as the Canterbury Festival wanted him to represent the Theatre Royal on their Council of Management. Having myself been retained on this Council of Management, having been told very firmly by Rosie Turner, that it was my right and that they wanted me to stay on this board. I magnanimously offered to accompany the young man who was my successor to his first meeting and we had a drink afterwards. He told me quite honestly that he had never run a theatre before and I thought I don't believe this. They have not only wasted money on the theatre but they have appointed an intelligent theatrical guy who has never run a theatre so what exactly is going on? I could see Sarah Thorne Theatre ticket sales going up and my old theatre going down and this was in no disrespect to the current Theatre Royal director. The Arts Committee wanted a totally different approach since apart from The Gang Show, they had out priced all the amateurs and no sensible drama had been brought in and the pantomime had been re-constituted as a 'Christmas Production'. In this offering the artists were also the musicians, which has been tried and failed in the commercial theatre and was not pantomime; so here was another example of running things entirely the wrong way. They were also paying out for productions to go in which I would never have done. For instance, to install a show the cost might be £1,000 for which you would only take £500 and consequently make a loss. Such a scenario of constant losses could only continue for a limited time. David Rankin was expedient in getting the first annual report for the next financial year and we noted the remarks about the Pratley Consultants that their Theatre Royal business plan was not working. Also mentioned in the annual return to Companies House which is in public domain; was that prior to the sale, the theatre was doing financially better than had been indicated in the Pratley Plan. This was indeed some solace for me. That plan was headed; 'The Death of the Showman!' would be contradicted in the longer term, since that showman was to be very much alive and kicking!

The Trust had had to re-mould their tactics by getting through more and more money from the grants and quite unnecessarily. Inevitably this would show a downward spiral in the viability of the business and I immediately saw my endowment fund going and no one would give me any answers. For each of the next four years you could see money being lost although it was not obvious where and what productions were not making money. On the other hand, they were doing awfully good art? or, so they thought! As to the endowment fund we had had a lump sum left to us by the Theatre Royal Chatham Trust and had elected to spend some of this on the building but keep back £60,000, to start a fund to pay us interest for the 'pension pot.' This had been spent within the first two years! Furthermore, during this period, I also noted problems in that the first Finance Director they appointed left and the new appointee had changed the accountants. These accountants had been employed by us for many years and were extremely strict and had never allowed anything that was unusual, as far as the records were concerned. They were suddenly asked to go which sent alarm bells going with me and several other people, however by now there were only two of the original trustees remaining. One who became the chairman and an architect, who was still peddling his plans about undertaking a complete restoration of the Theatre Royal. All the other trustees were new.

In my view here was a classic case of an inexperienced theatre chap putting on shows he may have liked, to please the Arts Council, all of which were losing money. It was obviously getting to the point that they needed almost constant extra funding in order to keep the theatre going at all and were drawing down grants in advance on the next year, which was a procedure that had to end somewhere. This it did after five years when a load of articles appeared in the local press about the council saying 'No', and I later found out that one of the councillors had said, 'Enough is enough we are taking the theatre back from the trust!' A number of us tried to obtain copies of the final accounts but a brick wall appeared from the authorities and the files have never been released.

There was also a very interesting letter by a guy called Wheatley (not me) in the local press, having a go about me for offering my services to help. However, the late Jeffrey Fendell, who was a most experienced fundraiser and local amateur actor, asked me if he could write a reply in public and it was in fact a masterful letter for which I was extremely grateful. He pointed out the truth that when I ran the theatre it was with my own money and in sensible hands, whereas now in his opinion the theatre's finances had been completely and utterly mismanaged. This had exposed what had actually happened and not only did I see people on the Arts Council getting the sack for making the decisions but also local arts officers as well. Could it be that politicians realised that they had been rumbled and that some people's heads had to roll?

The way I had advocated how the Theatre Royal should have been run had I remained, was the format I also used for setting up the Sarah Thorne Theatre which had now really started to climb. For whilst the Theatre Royal went down, we went from one show a month to one per weekend and then two. We brought back the summer Season and also re-introduced pantomime having tried Christmas Shows. We also helped re-open the Granville at Ramsgate with a Christmas show 'Mother Goose' in 2007, which we repeated in 2008 with the help of Michael Harradine who had the distinction of being the only successful operator at Manston Airport with his company, Invicta Airways.

The Granville owned by the council was bought by a lot of local individuals who wanted to keep it going by reverting it back to a theatre, as opposed to a cinema. Sarah Thorne Theatre was to rise significantly when we put on 'Scrooge' the pantomime. We have over a number of years financed shows without borrowing money, by paying strict attention to cash flow and receiving low pay ourselves, which was the same format as I would have continued at the Theatre Royal and this has been noticed by so many people. For example, the new Chairman of the Arts Council Sir Peter Bazalgette, was so impressed by what he had seen he thought we would be a model of how to operate local theatres for the future. (Sir Peter was the Great great grandson of Sir Joseph Bazalgate who planned the 1,300-mile network of Victorian sewers in the 1860s, to prevent untreated sewerage being flushed into the River Thames.)

Gaining Three Valued Patrons

Dame Judi Dench said 'Yes' after an introduction from David Languish which hit the headlines and people started to take us even more seriously. Most important was that we had proved that if you run this old theatre in Broadstairs in a business-like way you can make it work. David Suchet was remarkable as he was in a play at the Apollo Theatre London and I had one of my 'psychic thoughts!' I had been at this theatre myself in my formative years. I wrote to him and asking whether he would be interested in being the actor patron as Dame Judi Dench was the actress patron and to my delight, he also said 'Yes!', because he was partly brought up in Birchington. I don't think that Dame Judi Dench has any local associations with this area. However, when I was introduced to Julian Fellows at a function at the RAF Club in Piccadilly, the chairman of the Noel Coward Charitable Trust, mentioned that I ran this theatre in Broadstairs where he explained he had spent his school holidays. I wrote to him and he kindly agreed to become our third patron.

A Message from a Fly on the Wall

After a couple of years, I had a tip off from a council employee who said I wish you had been at the meeting when the licensing authorities said to a group of politicians, 'We wish to report on a disastrous drop in standards at the Theatre Royal Margate since the previous management went'. There was a whole list of things not done such as leaving chains on the doors and one of the councillors was actually heard saying, 'What the 'f' did we do?' They knew then as I knew after three years that they had made a total mistake. On recent reflection I think that opening the Sarah Thorne was a way of galvanising some very good staff in a different location, because I had every intention of staying a producer in the knowledge that I had the money independently to be able to do this. I was now at a stage in life when I had no wish to transplant my roots elsewhere and to continue in theatre at Sarah Thorne just fell naturally into place. Although some of my colleagues have found other jobs and have gone, the seeds are still there. Of course, it does not have the raked auditorium of the Theatre Royal opened in the late 1700s and is a functional building. Whatever effort you are putting into it you are doing in order to bring about change and of course it is the quality of what you are offering that brings in the audience. This was summed up very nicely by an Italian lady friend, when she came to see 'The Mystery of Edwin Drood' in 2014. She said, 'Michael, when you come into London to see me you see a product in the theatre, a product which is obviously intended to make money, for as a product this is what it has to do. Down here this is real theatre. You are actually all mucking in and doing things and putting on what the locals want to see!' This perspective illustrates my thoughts that there are few theatres like the Sarah Thorne which we must continue to nurture, since we can only put on productions in a particular way which is different from even the Theatre Royal. The beauty of Hilderstone is that it has a multifunctional performing area, in which seating can be arranged to suit the production. If I had to depend on the standard auditorium seating, fifty percent of the product just wouldn't happen. Seating can be arranged for a piano concert, theatre in the round and table seating for cabaret shows and that flexibility is very re-assuring. If I had both these theatres under one management, I could run them far better than I could have done before, because with this synergy, we would create 'joint ventures'. Sarah Thorne is not only a versatile 'fringe theatre' or studio, it is also the nurturing ground for non-professionals whom as soon as they start taking money can move up to the Theatre Royal. The Theatre Royal can still do its tribute shows and its pantomime and some of the big operas and ballets that we cannot undertake at the less spacious Sarah Thorne, but one management could control both.

The Future for the Sarah Thorne at Hilderstone

Here is a centre with a priority for teaching and the revenue is coming in. As for actors performing there it is a very different challenge to the Theatre Royal Margate. At the moment the Sarah Thorne has a very small management staff but most important is that it is only open two days per week, plus educational holidays, which is probably all you need in Broadstairs. We have been noticing a growing trend that most of the business is on the Sunday afternoon matinees because of a larger number of seniors who don't like coming out at night. The beauty of Hilderstone is that it is let out five days per week to adult education and it is this income that overall helps support the theatre building itself. Having such a small staff and relatively low overheads enables us to continue to pay our way. The trick is not to buy shows in and do them at risk and of course we still make money out of the bar. There are of course drawbacks in all this since it means that at least two people have to come in and voluntary staff have to be found for the weekend. Seating has also to be put out for the shows. The bar has to be monitored and continuously kept stocked up. Everything has to be taken out of cupboards and put back again after every performance as a consequence of converting the small hall into a bar area. In long runs like the Summer Rep season, we have to dismantle some of the set for just one night, for something else which has to go on stage by contract during the day and then put it back together again. Although this makes it very labour-intensive it keeps the theatre as a 'working theatre'. There are many other ways I have discovered to keep the theatre going without much added subsidy. The long term of all this is that we are under discussion with Kent County Council for a proper lease as they are aware that they have spent very little money on this building for the last few years. We still intend to experiment and try things out for new audiences and also continue to use it for local amateurs which is the reason for our own in-house company, 'The Hilderstone Players, Hilderstone Musical Society', as well as have a Christmas production and continue to run it as an on-going theatre.

The Survival of Local Theatre Depends Upon Volunteers

If we get in enough money it would be nice to start an apprenticeship scheme, so we can train theatre managers and technicians as well as theatre programmers. Taking a leaf out of Douglas Byng's book, 'don't stay on the stage too long in advanced years forgetting my lines and breaking wind!' I would like to pass down a number of my duties to a younger generation and still keep my mind active in later years by retaining others. This is my current long-term perspective for the Sarah Thorne Theatre at the Hilderstone Centre. When you look outside of the main conurbations such as big cities like Manchester, Birmingham and London, there are still a lot of places which can support a local theatre that will keep people interested. There are many little theatres which belong to the 'Little Theatre Guild of Great Britain' such as the Crescent Theatre, Birmingham, the Prospect Theatre and the Tavistock Theatre Company (London), now with their own theatre in Stoke Newington London N16. I often remind the youth of today that you might well love the theatre, but you won't necessarily make any money out of it!

You might have to accept perhaps a lowly paid job or a higher one such as a bank manager or doctor, but if you really want to be in theatre keep in the non-professional theatre. We need to upmarket this more because as is often discussed, these non-professional 'fiefdoms' sometimes don't advertise or have auditions. I tend to look at my job more and more as nothing different to a railway preservation society. You have lots of volunteers but you have to have a couple of people who are handling the Health and Safety, the finances and the overall control. You must not forget that those volunteers will get an enormous amount of satisfaction from that experience. Valuable volunteers who helped me some previously at the Theatre Royal as well as the Sarah Thorne Theatre, the previously mentioned Ronnie Cox, Helen Waddington, Susan Laverick, Jay Thomas, Sheila Burke and Jane Fitzgerald. In a Railway Preservation Society volunteers might just clean carriages or oil the engine but when they see it all in motion working in the presence of public interest such as with steam locomotives, then they can say 'I have played a part in that!' From my own experience I may not have been a big producer but I have occasionally put money into a show and I think, well at the moment I only own half a percent of The Full Monty but that is marvellous because I have helped to keep that show on the road! One lady volunteer has said to me, 'I now look forward to my week-ends because I can come into the theatre and do a job and it tires me out for three or four hours, but for the rest of the week I am getting over it and looking forward to the next!' Therefore, it is also about helping people in their old age and keeping them going and interested in real life projects. Volunteers are very vital people in a community who must not be over exploited by any establishment. For instance, the people who go into hospitals and talk to patients, who wouldn't normally have anyone to talk to. That is a very valuable volunteering job and a very good use of the lives of those no longer in full time employment. As for this site we would like to improve it again by having a fly-tower for scenery and a store in which to keep it on the premises. Also, a separate bar and raked seating. For this you can have a sort of 'stadium seating' that can actually be stacked permanently at the rear of the auditorium and wheeled out as and when required. Such things of course will take years to raise the funding for. I am amazed when people come to me who haven't been for say, two years, and say that they are already seeing changes. The latest development for us is online bookings. The website is there of course but in need of constant improvement particularly with the youth that are emerging who are able to do this.

Call for New Play Writers

As the Theatre Manager I would also like to encourage more youth to do some 'sensible' play writing. The reason we have to keep reviving things is the same for the contemporary art movement in galleries like Turner. There is the occasional one object which is good and the rest really rubbish. We used to have a repertory system where you tried out plays and they were re-named and went into London where they became hits. Then went back out and toured again and we lack that now. There are people who just cannot construct plays although there is some very good writing out there and John Goodrum composes his murder play every year which is quality new writing. In 2016 the Rattigan Society promoted a competition for playwriting and the successful play 'The Onion at the End' was premièred at the Sarah Thorne in February 2018, which was a two act play and lasted no more than seventy-five minutes with no more than six characters.

Reflecting on Theatre Director Michael's Personal Health.

A little background on my private health is that I discovered at eighteen after my medical for the ABC cinema apprenticeship scheme that I had high blood pressure and nothing was ever done about this until I married Terrie who has the sign of a 'green snake,' i.e.: interested in medical knowledge. The doctor said to me, 'Well, you are hyper-active and a businessman so you had better go on tablets!' At twenty-nine I had opened up my second shop and I was getting dizzy spells so I thought well, prevention is better than cure and I went to this lady doctor in Gerrards Cross who said to me, 'There is nothing wrong with you, you are a standard businessman and Michael, I have seen this over the years, but I will give you a little examination' and she said to me afterwards, 'Do you smoke?' I said, 'Yes'. She replied, 'What do you smoke?' and I said, 'Well, I can't stand cigarettes but I like Havana cigars, but as I 've got a cold at the moment I have dropped off them and also my favourite pipe tobacco, which was "'Baby's Bottom'", by a firm called 'Savourys', although they have now stopped making it. So I am not smoking at the moment due to a cold.' and she said, 'Oh, can you give up smoking because it is very injurious to health and although you don't inhale the smoke, the nicotine still gets into the system.' So I said "Yes!" 'and gave up the same day. I had a cigar offered to me a month later which I actually threw away because I just couldn't take it and I haven't smoked since. At the same medical examination, she had said, 'Do you like a drink?' I said, 'Well, yes I like a little drop' and in those days it was brandy or whisky and the occasional real ale. So she said, 'You can carry on drinking if you give up smoking but don't have bottles of the stuff, do it at the end of the day, it is better than all these pills us doctors give you!' So that I did which lasted me from the age of thirty for twenty years when my wife said to me, 'I think that you ought to have a man medical' when they said 'You'd better have tablets for blood pressure'. This was unavoidable. So I am legally entitled to drink because I gave up smoking. Every year I go for tests for the liver etc and they take samples of blood. I never go into excessive drinking and if you are driving you cannot do both. Mind you, when theatricals come to visit the bottle is out! Usually I never have more than two or three glasses per night, so I don't consider I am drinking to excess. This is just a little story to let people know that you are allowed to drink but not smoke and after quoting a now famous saying by Marie Lloyd, 'As I always say... a little of what you fancy does you good!'

Chapter 8 - The Way Ahead

In 2016 a number of events happened which might have implications on the years ahead. At a personal level my wife Terrie was diagnosed as having a minor cancer in the intestines which meant that she was now to become the main priority in my life. As the Theatre Royal had been put out to tender by the council, Matthew Quirk of the Merry Opera Company, who was looking for a theatre base, asked me and Michael Harridine, the retired owner of Invicta Airways based at Manston Kent, if we could join forces in order to undertake this tender. He also had theatrical connections. We were shown the trading figures and a site visit was arranged. Curiously enough during that site visit Jay Thomas, now my fellow director at the Sarah Thorne Broadstairs, was to point out that by putting my spectacles in front of the oil painting of Sarah Thorne, the facial image was similar, which to this day I still find spooky! I asked the Conservation Officer if there were grants available to restore the theatre. His reply was very interesting. He said, 'After all the lies that have been told... no!' I stood on that stage with Jay looking at the exquisite auditorium saying to myself, after ten years I have now been proved right and I have won, since the figures had revealed that in those ten years since I had left the Theatre Royal, my trading figures had not been beaten and a lot of money had been misspent on the building. I thought to myself, do I really want to come back again and re-invent the wheel? I did however cover my back by personally telling Chris Wells, the then Leader of the Thanet District Council, that I would always be happy to operate in an advisory capacity. Although it later transpired that Council Officers during a points meeting had decided to go with a large London-based contemporary theatre having access to grants. Ironically Matthew Quirk and I were told afterwards that we had come number two in the listings, being considered the most commercially minded! The third and final pointer for the future was that two directors of the Sarah Thorne, Gordon Eyles and David Rankin, stated their intention to leave at the end of the year 2016. Consequently, this left just me and Jay Thomas, who had been the technical director since the opening of our Sarah Thorne venture. I now faced a conundrum as I did not want to retire early like my father, but wanted to remain in some capacity in the theatre for as long as I possibly could. Apart from this my now sole partner Jay Thomas was also the owner of his own electrical business and had limited time in which to offer his support. We therefore decided to re-allocate all directorial duties at Sarah Thorne to make our respective lives easier through the greater application of information technology, to modernise the whole business administration. Since I was now financially self-sufficient I informed Jay that as he was younger, I would make sure he had the lion's share of any remuneration.

I was also keen to build a younger team to pass down my experience to eventually enable them to take over completely when I finally retired! These turning points actually made me very happy as I could continue staging productions with Michael Friend and John Goodrum, allowing me more time than I have ever had to enjoy what is laughingly called 'a private life'. In the spring of 2017 I was contemplating eleven productions in the next year, including the staging of the Terrance Rattigan award winning play, 'The Onion at the End'.

From left to right: David Suchet CBE, Barbara Longford (Chairman), Michael Wheatley-Ward (Theatre Liason), Princess George Galitzine MBE (President), Julian Fellowes

Poirot actor DAVID SUCHET and Downton Abbey creator JULIAN FELLOWES are amongst four judges for a new play award to honour Sir Terence Rattigan's unique contribution to British drama.

The Terence Rattigan Society Award is one of the few given for a new play for the theatre. The award winner will receive £2,500 and the play will be guaranteed a professional production of no less than six performances at the Sarah Thorne Theatre in Kent in the Summer of 2017. Equally attractive is the second prize of £1,000 and a guaranteed rehearsed reading. The other judges are director, Thea Sharrock and academic and Rattigan expert, Professor Dan Rebellato.

Welcoming the award, David Suchet said: "I'm thrilled that the Terence Rattigan Society is offering an award for a new play in his name. As one of this country's true masters of the dramatists' craft, it is a fitting tribute to his enormous contribution to the theatre".

His fellow judge Julian Fellowes commented: "Terence Rattigan is one of England's greatest playwrights whose light was hidden under a bushel for far too long before his recent rediscovery. An award in his name, dedicated to finding new talent and bringing it out of the darkness for the public to enjoy, seems only fitting."

Premier cast of 'The Onion at the end' End' Left to right Lainey Shaw, Alexander Hulme, Johanna Pearson-Farr, David Suchet, Clive Greenwood, Julian Fellowes, Stephen Martin-Bradley and Edward Broomfield (Photo: Giles Cole)

The Newsletter of the Terence Rattigan Society in April 2018 (Issue No 4) featured an article by Hazel Keer reporting on the winning play's Broadstairs premiere at the Sarah Thorne Theatre. This was Roy Kendall's 'Onion at the End' which was attended by the Rattigan Society's President Sir David Suchet also a patron of the Sarah Thorne theatre and Julian Fellowes vice president and patron. The third patron, Dame Judi Dench was unable to attend but others present were Greta Scacchi and Geoffrey Wansell. The play is set in Southport during the Depression and follows the fortunes of two end-of-the-pier performers who are boarding with a determined landlady Rose Hoskins who has an ailing son Teddy. Hazel Kerr described the set as naturalistic and Michael Friend's direction as sensitive. The play focuses on the lack of success of the two performers which is attributed, by the theatre owner Dan, as due to poor timing. He insists that they adopt a rhyming technique which eventually bears fruit. After the performance a buffet tea was laid on by the volunteer staff with the opportunity to meet the cast.

Members of the Volunteer Support Staff (Andi Vigo Stage Manager. Sarah lighting and sound, Jay Thomas, Michael and Terri Wheatley-Ward, Jane Fitzgerald and Sheila Burke) with David Suchet and Julian Fellowes

Being a fatalist Michael now looks forward with eagerness to what the future might hold with an assurance that having survived in the theatre for over fifty years, he would like to continue for another fifty.... God willing!

During his ten years at Hilderstone's Sarah Thorne Theatre he notes that there have been various proposals which have so far not been processed into action plans. For instance, some four years ago having done so well at the Sarah Thorne Theatre we were asked by the Council to consider that as they wanted to dispose of the premises, they could let us have it for £1 if we formed our own trust, which is just what we did. However, much has happened since then with local financial affairs requiring cut-backs. Adult education at the Hilderstone Centre is being hived off as a separate entity of course requiring premises in which to function. The council are now reiterating that as they still own the building and 'adult education' should have the theatre in which to run their classes in week days, but the theatre should have an office of its own (i.e. a Box Office), which it now has, enabling it to operate as a small business enterprise.

The theatre volunteers are still involved at the weekends. This has been a considerable advance since previously with a temporary box office in the main building which served other purposes as well. This new box office area enables us to have access to the files and is a working office. Importantly however there are still so many unknown factors preventing the development of a strategic plan for the theatre and the Hilderstone Centre as a whole. Christopher Wells, originally the conservative candidate for Cliftonville as well as St Peter's Town Council, has helped over the years with fund-raising. Thanks should also be given to Jeff Kirkpatrick, ex leader of the council, councillor Alan Marsh and Councillor Rosalind Binks for their continuous support. Michael has always been an advocate of 'teamwork' and for some time at the Sarah Thorne has had Andi Vigo who actually came out of retirement, to help him out, which she would not do for anyone else, the reason being that she loves being involved, although she is currently not a well woman herself. This illustrates the importance of having a team spirit ('esprit de corps'), or a group of people who enjoy working together and over a period of time. This includes those previously mentioned Richard Thomas, Jane Fitzgerald, Sheila Burke, Ronnie Cox, Helen Waddington and of course Michael's wife Terrie Wheatley-Ward. All this makes for a good 'Community Theatre'.

Personal Satisfaction and Reward

Michael now often reflects back to his first tour 'Murder by the Book' the first play, recalling that it was up and running only after a hell of a lot of work. He sat thinking, "Well, you've done it and the audience are loving it" and knew that it was my name and Marion Parks over the title as the producers. It didn't worry me that I wasn't on stage since I had achieved something for myself, which is an immense satisfaction which any director can feel. I had of course picked up directing much later after theatre management, largely through watching other directors and how they worked. For example, we had to resurrect 'The Farndale Avenue Murder Mystery' due to a week that was 'dark' at the Theatre Royal Margate. This was in 2003/4 and my wife Terrie was involved also and they said 'We have no one to direct this but Michael could!' I said, 'Well, I'll have a go' and that is how it came about. Everything was going wrong for instance, instead of the house tabs going up at the beginning of the second act then they came down. The greatest challenge was the chair sequence which eventually worked after much practice. I was so proud of this as my first production, I sat through it every night and an added bonus was that the press adored it. The truth is that you have got to be good to be bad and I thought, 'wonderful boy, you have done it!' As there were no training schemes in my younger days for theatre producers even in London, I had no proper guidance and as mentioned before I had to 'learn by doing' and 'trial and error'. I suppose with hindsight I could have written to a producer somewhere and asked to be taken in hand to work as an apprentice. Naturally I avoided going on stage as an ASM or an extra, because I never really liked 'acting'. I suppose that to be a good actor you have to be self-disciplined and listen to the director and I couldn't learn lines very well and in addition to this there were stage nerves. Contrastingly I never got nervous about operating the electric cues. Of course, most actors hopefully receive some kudos from the audience whereas a theatre manager does not get that first hand.

As a consequence, and as a living biography this could have no end so it would be appropriate to end here and now on a high!

Michael in the box office of the Sarah Thorne Theatre Broadstairs

Conclusion

Reflecting back on the career of Michael Wheatley-Ward, it is impossible not to make comparisons with Sarah Thorne, who encouraged and nurtured dedicated actors and undertook well tried and tested works, which eventually with her drama school, established her as an institution of quality. She was always prepared to take on new talent and encourage a culture of supporting working relationships as well as audience satisfaction. As a non-actor Michael has also followed these methods and states that he gets a great deal of comfort from seeing the audience enjoy the play. He even compares himself to Sir Oswald Stoll, who would sit in a box and attentively note the audience reaction to what was on stage. In his words, 'I did not want the applause myself because I am a 'party-giver' rather than a 'party-goer'. I have never wished to become a performer. At the present time a lot of people like musicals which are expensive to put on and a different game with me in the provinces than in the West End. In the latter they like a name of a play with a catchy title, although if we all knew the answer to what achieves box office success we would all be millionaires. Theatres need to take so many thousands a week in order to be viable which is what used to happen with Keith Prowse ticket agencies. You now have all these half-price ticket booths so people know that although the price is say, £65, if it is a struggling production you can get in at half price and there are plenty of places to buy these tickets. A show has to make say £80,000 per week to stay on. On the other hand, there are a lot of investors looking to reduce their taxes by contributing to 'lost leaders'. In America you have strings of producers clubbing together to put the money up and some of them are secretaries representing companies who have tax losses, but looking to lose money rather than gain it. Financing a production can be a very interesting game and I have myself invested in the odd show in London. As an 'angel' (a sponsor in theatrical terms), my small investment compared to the 'big fish', still makes me feel that I am contributing to keeping some people in employment. Peter Saunders always said to me 'if you say to your investors consider the money gone, you are being true to them because in many cases it probably has gone. Consequently, what sustains you in this is your retail business which was Douglas Byng's advice saying, 'get a business behind you!' I toured with two other producers on Geoffrey Archer's 'Beyond Reasonable Doubt' and on the third week we ran out of money because of the lack of cash flow, as previous theatres had not paid us what they owed. The show should have closed but we had another fifteen weeks to go.

So I went to the bank and on the strength of my name and the shop they paid the wages which were £10,000 for that week. We limped on with this production and in the end got fiddled by a theatre in Scotland, who allegedly had 'interpreted the contract differently'. This was a subsidised theatre in Glasgow and we even went to Geoffrey Archer who took it to cabinet level. Instead of getting a ten-thousand-pound guarantee against seventy percent of the box office which was close to £20,000, we only got the £10,000 guarantee and not the extra £4,000 that was due to us.

Consequently, we lost several thousands that week, nearly finishing the tour but when I complained to my management association, believe it or not the head of that association who knew the new Artistic Director at this opera house, sided with him on the issue. In the end the three producers had to personally find about two thousand each to rescue the tour, in addition to having the creative and arduous role of the production. In this case the whole experience of working with a state-run opera company left a bad taste in the mouth. The lack of cash flow in this example was in my view was through not honouring an agreement as well as the lack of prompt payment. As a result, I didn't hang around long which meant the end of my membership of a management association. Importantly not considered here seems to be the legal issue of the Law of Contract in which there is 'an offer' and an 'acceptance' in order to be a legally binding situation, on which neither party could renegade without appropriate compensation. Why they were allowed to get away with it is one of the mysteries of theatre finance which can give us all a bad name.

We played one particular circuit with **'Beyond Reasonable Doubt'**, where we had different levels of box office receipts such as seventy percent to us and thirty to the theatre, eighty twenty, sixty forty and so on, depending on the location of that particular theatre. When we investigated one of our investors, a large stock-broker, said, 'Do you know where it has gone wrong? You have never got any more than fifty percent of the box office, even though you were entitled to between seventy and eighty percent!' The 'charge-backs' by theatres for publicity, staff (i.e. contras), are adjusted resulting in the theatre always getting fifty percent of the box office and a pure 'fiddle'. Unfortunately, a lot of this still goes on assisted by box office booking fees and restoration fees. For me this is iniquitous which is why commercial theatre has sometimes been given a bad name. I was determined when we ran our theatres not to go down that road. The only person I know who has ever applied restoration fees properly is Cameron Mackintosh as he has spent a fortune on his theatres.

Some Further Experiences and Tribulations of Theatre Finance.

On self-analysis, it is true to say that I took things by chance and of course some went wrong. What was crucially important was having the belief that something will turn up or happen, which is how I have conducted myself throughout my working life which seems to tell me has been successful. You have some ability even a 'sixth sense' to go for things which you know are going to be achievable. I have always believed in this and my wife Terrie has recently verified, that 'If you get an idea go for it otherwise you will regret not doing it later on'.

I don't have any regrets over the things which I have done, particularly if you learn by experience not to make the same mistake again. Lew Grade used to say 'The only way to make money is to lose it in the first place'. The theatre world however, has changed irrevocably from when I started at the tender age of sixteen. On my return back to live theatre in 1985, in those twenty years some remarkable changes had occurred. We experienced local authorities buying theatres from the old circuits and trying to run them with public money and making big losses. Local authorities are subject to political changes at the next election, thereby reducing the call for consistent and universally accepted strategic plans. Consequently, it is short-termism which prevails and which history demonstrates because theatre projects such as the Theatre Royal are more precarious. In more recent years we have gone full circle with some local authorities leasing theatres back to private enterprise or undertaking joint ventures, between public and private institutions. This has resulted in bringing in all sorts of different deals and different ways of running them. Michael's view is that live entertainment will still win through although with the major limitation, that it is manpower constrained. A cinema of course brings your actors in a can and does not give you the problem of interpersonal relationships in a theatre where you are dealing with so many people's egos and insecurities.

From an entirely different aspect what is the cost to an audience of going to the theatre as opposed to the cinema or staying at home watching television? Well some cinemas now cost only £10 per seat to see a film and in my present theatre, the Sarah Thorne Broadstairs; I can put on plays for that price, although the work involvement in live theatre is completely different. You are getting to the point now where the repertory system has virtually gone because no one today will put up with what we used to go along with in terms of the long hours which just had to be put in. For example, we have the Summer Repertory Season currently at the Sarah Thorne and I and Michael Friend will work seven twelve-hour days for four weeks, by the end of which time we will be completely exhausted. However, we will have put on four plays, a couple of which will go on tour, as was the norm in the 1950s and '60s. You would not get anyone to do this now because there are a lot of people in theatre who are literally there with stars in their eyes and just want to be a star. They see it as a move to another career and consequently dedicated theatre folk are now few and far between. People like Cameron Mackintosh deserve more than they have got because they put their money back into the theatre which they believed in. There are many people today who just think 'it would be nice to make money out of it and you can't always do this'. I am a firm believer that if you put on what people want to see they'll come in and see it. If you get the prices right then you can subsidise the non-popular productions for the minorities like opera and ballet and still make this work as well. To suss out what people want and what they will come to see is what it has always been which is experimenting with differing theatrical experiences.

Acknowledgements

The biographer wishes to express his grateful thanks to Sir Alistair Hunter for his preface for this book.

To Marnie Summerfield and Tom Cull for their suggestions.

To Felicity McMAHON of 5RB Coutts Bank 5, Gray's Inn Square London WC1 R 5AH for examining this manuscript for possible libel and legal issues.

To Gordon Clarkson for his information and advice, pictures of productions and programmes and his experience at the Theatre Royal Margate.

To Veronica (Ronnie) Cox for relating her experience over some years at the Theatre Royal in a voluntary capacity.

To James Bellamy and Peter Such for their diligent and painstaking editing throughout the compilation of this work

Michael Wheatley-Ward wishes to thank his wife Terrie for her guidance throughout the four years of preparation of this book.

Also to past and present business partners – Gordon Rippington, Brian Winterbourne, Jay Thomas and all the volunteers of the Theatre Royal Margate and Sarah Thorne Theatre Broadstairs.

Lightning Source UK Ltd.
Milton Keynes UK
UKHW020013260921
391126UK00001B/31